How Pornography
HARMS

What Today's Teens, Young Adults, Parents, and Pastors Need to Know

John D. Foubert, Ph.D.

Trademark notice: Product or corporate names may be trademarks or registered trademarks, and are used only for identification and explanation without intent to infringe.

LifeRich Publishing is a registered trademark of The Reader's Digest Association, Inc.

LifeRich Publishing books may be ordered through booksellers or by contacting:

LifeRich Publishing
1663 Liberty Drive
Bloomington, IN 47403
www.liferichpublishing.com
1 (888) 238-8637

ISBN: 978-1-4897-1023-9 (sc)
ISBN: 978-1-4897-1024-6 (hc)
ISBN: 978-1-4897-1022-2 (e)

Library of Congress Control Number: 2016917749

Print information available on the last page.

LifeRich Publishing rev. date: 11/18/2016

Contents

Endorsements

How Pornography Harms fills a big need in our fight against pornography. There are a great many books that tell us why the Christian community should be against pornography, but John Foubert provides the intelligent reasons to fight the battle and supplies the ammunition to conquer this devastating issue.

Josh D. McDowell, Author/Speaker

Foubert artfully weaves extensive research with unvarnished testimony to expose the sordid and ever more violent reality of modern pornography. His convincing clarion-call is for society to wake up to how the skyrocketing internet use of pornography is ruining lives and degrading women. The text is an important read for any community leader, family member or friend.

Dr. Stephen Beers
Vice President for Student Development, Athletics and
Facilities Services at John Brown University
Chair, Student Development Commission, Council
for Christian Colleges and Universities

This book is about an unsettling truth, one that requires immediate attention from all advocates of social justice, regardless of their particular faith. John Foubert's analysis is an important tool for those seeking to get involved in the ongoing struggle to curb one of the world's most compelling social problems. He should be commended for "telling us like it is" and for his never ending dedication to eliminating pornographic materials from our lives.

Walter S. DeKeseredy, Ph.D.
Anna Deane Carlson Chair of Social Sciences
Director of the Research Center on Violence, West Virginia University

The wide-spread use of pornography is harmful to individuals, marriages, and those involved in the porn industry. Research clearly documents the physiological and emotional ramifications associated with pornography use. This highly potent digital drug is destroying lives and families. It is time for all of us to be educated about the harmful effects of pornography and take a stand to protect children and those who are unaware. Dr. Foubert is a world-leader and academic in this area. This book is an important reference that all need to read.

Andrew Doan, MD, PhD
Commander, U.S. Navy
Head, Dept. of Mental Health Addictions & Resilience Research
Naval Medical Center San Diego

Pornography has morphed into a ubiquitous assault on human dignity, with the Internet providing a vehicle presenting this supernormal stimulus with limitless novelty. Dr. John Foubert has accurately described the harm and toxicity pornography wreaks upon individuals and couples, and presents the perspective not only of scholars, but also of those directly affected. This book not only provides a warning, but also offers solutions we would do well to follow in addressing what has become the major public health crisis of our time.

Donald Hilton, M.D.
Neurosurgeon and Chief, Department of Surgery,
Stone Oak Methodist Hospital
Author, Pornography Addiction: A Neuroscience Perspective

Pornography is a pandemic plague wreaking untold havoc. This well-written, well-researched book is a powerful prescription. Dr. Foubert hits the issue from all sides, including the biblical, spiritual dimension, and gives hope and practical help for avoiding and overcoming this spiritual cancer. Every person, especially every Christian, needs to be armed with the truth in this book. Read it, apply it, and pass it on to others.

Dr. Mark Hitchcock
Associate Professor of Bible Exposition, Dallas Theological Seminary
Senior Pastor, Faith Bible Church in Edmond, OK

In comprehensively reviewing a rapidly growing literature on the enormous pornography industry, John Foubert has provided a compelling argument that the on-line sexually explicit media now ubiquitously available is a source of environmental pollution that has the potential to harm nearly everyone with whom it comes into contact, perhaps with the exception of those who reap huge profits from compromising the sexualities of users and performers. As the author points out, there is now considerable evidence of the link between pornography consumption and real-world violence. And as with all violent media, its effects are subtle, cumulative, and indirect. *How Pornography Harms* is essential reading for anyone who is concerned about the numerous social issues connected with the distribution of this demeaning material.

Christopher Kilmartin, Ph.D.
Emeritus Professor of Psychological Science
University of Mary Washington

How Pornography Harms is a wake-up call for society and the church. If Dr. Foubert is right, and I think he is, we must have the courage to tackle the issue of pornography head on. This book is a must-read for anyone who cares about the health of individuals, families, and our culture as a whole. Pick up a copy, read it, and help spread the word.

Sean McDowell, Ph.D.
Professor, Biola University
Best-selling author of more than twenty books
including *A New Kind of Apologist*.

John is one of the courageous experts who places the issue of pornography in America front and center. Today, the subject is overwhelming, complicated, and politically incorrect – yet absolutely devastating to an entire generation worldwide. I applaud this book! Straightforward, well researched and practical for families.

Dave Riner, Executive Director, Student Mobilization

How Porn Harms sounds the alarm for parents, counselors, educators, and pastors alike who continue to be naive to pornography's devastating effects on our children and our culture. Dr. Foubert balances scientific research with personal narratives to create an engaging and enlightening portrayal of a national epidemic. I highly recommend the book and commend Dr. Foubert for his ongoing work to raise awareness on this subject.

-Jon Ritner, Lead Pastor, Ecclesia Hollywood
ChurchInHollywood.com

The title of this book says it all, pornography harms. Pornography is a disease in our culture, and as an educator and a parent, I am concerned that it is largely going untreated. John Foubert's new book, *How Pornography Harms* is part of the prescription for fighting the spread of this disease. This book will shock you into awareness and prepare you to help cure and prevent pornography's impact on our youth. If you care about the coming generations, this is a must read.

Dr. Skip Trudeau
Vice President for Student Development
Taylor University

Dr. Foubert's collection of research and insights into today's porn culture will smack you in the face with one cold hard fact: porn harms. It doesn't harm a few, some, or many. It harms all. Pornography has changed our society and Foubert unassailably documents that there is nothing positive in the result.

Patrick A. Trueman
President & CEO, National Center on Sexual Exploitation

About the Author

John D. Foubert, Ph.D. is Principal of John D. Foubert, LLC (www.johnfoubert.com), National President of One in Four (www.oneinfourusa.org) and Professor of Higher Education and Student Affairs at Oklahoma State University. He earned his undergraduate degree with a double major in Psychology and Sociology from the College of William and Mary, his Master's degree in Psychology from the University of Richmond, and his Ph.D. in College Student Personnel Administration from the University of Maryland at College Park.

Dr. Foubert is an interdisciplinary scholar with over 50 peer-reviewed publications. He has written seven books about the prevention of sexual violence and two about managing life in college residence halls. *How Pornography Harms* is his 10th book, and the one he hopes will have the broadest impact on society.

Dr. Foubert has testified before Congress and has been called upon by the White House and the Pentagon for his expertise in rape prevention. He speaks and consults with colleges, churches, high schools, and the military about the harms of pornography and how to end sexual violence. He regularly appears in the national media in outlets such as CNN, World Magazine, NPR, The New York Times, The Atlantic, The Houston Chronicle, and U.S. News and World Report. Dr. Foubert blogs for the Huffington Post. He has given over 200 professional presentations to conferences, universities, community and military organizations worldwide.

At the age of 19, Dr. Foubert spoke with Josh McDowell prior to a large public gathering, then heard him talk to 1,000 people on what it meant to be born again. Thanks to that, and the providence of God, John then gave his life to Christ. He has been following Him imperfectly ever since. He lives in Oklahoma City with his family.

Dr. Foubert tweets about the harms of pornography, ending sexual violence, and Christian living @JohnFoubert. You can visit his website at www.johnfoubert.com and email him at john.foubert@gmail.com.

Acknowledgements

As a follower of Jesus, I acknowledge that nothing I do is possible without Him. I hold to the theory that no book is written alone, regardless of whose name appears on the cover. I am indebted to many people who have either directly or indirectly made this book possible. I wish to acknowledge so many, and apologize up front for those I inadvertently left out.

First, I thank Donald Craig, who lit my fire to understand pornography for the wretched evil that it is. Don brought the topic up with me frequently, and at first I thought he was being way too dramatic and extreme. When he brought it up, it made me uncomfortable. And then I studied pornography, I saw it for the evil that it is, and saw that Don was absolutely right. Thank you, Don, for pointing me in that direction and for sharing your story with me many years ago. I hope this book will have the kind of impact that I know you hope it will. I hope that in sharing this book, I will be able to afflict the comfortable, just as you afflicted me years ago.

Thank you Andre Durham, my trusted and capable doctoral advisee, without whom this book would not have been completed. Andre copy edited every chapter, provided ideas about each, and made the text far more readable. He provided invaluable feedback as a neutral reader who has a rich talent for the written word. Thank you, Andre! I look forward to many joint writing projects in the future, and to watching your career unfold. Thanks also to Traci Hudgin for conducting several interviews with female participants for this book. I'm so glad you discovered a love for qualitative research through this project! Clearly, you have a very bright future ahead.

Thank you to all the scholars who so generously shared their time with me. To a person, each one offered to schedule additional time beyond the hour or more they were kind enough to share with me. I have learned so much from them. As I share what they taught me throughout this book, I hope you learn from them as well. Dr. Ana Bridges, I admire your work tremendously, and consider it an honor to have published articles with you about this subject. I particularly appreciate your intellectual integrity and methodological dexterity. Thank you for your groundbreaking research and for continuing to use your gifts to discover such useful knowledge. Thank you so much Dr. Walter DeKeseredy. Your cheerful demeanor and willingness to respond to every question I have is something I am deeply grateful for – thank you! Your theoretical work in ending men's violence against women stands out among all others; thank you for all you do.

Dr. Gail Dines, your passion for fighting pornography with every fiber of your being, regardless of the personal consequences, inspires me on the deepest level. I most appreciate your insight into the finances of the business we are taking on, and your advice on preparing my loved ones for this book's release. Thank you for your selfless service to humanity. Dr. Donald Hilton, thank you for providing me a deeper understanding of how the brain works, and how that intersects with pornography use. Thank you also for your advice about publishers, and for being willing to go to bat for me.

Dr. Mark Hitchcock, I have never met a more learned theologian who can translate the Bible with such intellectual dexterity. Your understanding of scripture is surpassed only by your humility. Thank you for your candor, your help in thinking of ways to raise awareness about this book, and for providing an integral perspective for it! Dr. Bob Jensen, I have admired your work for a long time. It was a thrill to be able to interview you in person, as much as Skype is personal anyway. Your thinking about pornography has the most clarity and insight I've ever heard. Thank you for all you have done to form the foundation of this area of study. I am indebted to you, as are so many who work in the broad movement to curtail the influence of the pornography industry.

Dr. Mary Anne Layden, you are a force of nature. Not only are you uncommonly able to see the seamless links in this area of study, you say them more quickly and with the sharpest wit of anyone I've met! It took quite awhile to transcribe my interview with you, as it was so rich and deep. You personify a scholar practitioner. Thank you for your impact. Dr. William Struthers, our meeting was obviously a God thing. I'm so glad we had the chance to visit while I was at Wheaton; I look forward to collaborating in some research and writing in the future!

January Villarubia, your sheer guts to share every bit of your ordeal with the industry and your resilience in life is an inspiring tale all should hear. I hope that I have honored your experience in this book, and that fewer will find themselves in the same circumstances as a result. Dr. Rebecca Whisnant, you are a brave scholar. I deeply appreciate how you approach your thinking and your writing. Bob Jensen told me you are one of the best scholars in this field; I agree. Dr. Paul Wright, your sheer volume of research in such a short period of time is both inspiring and daunting. Thank you for all you are giving, and no doubt will continue to provide, to the study of sexually explicit media.

I am deeply indebted to the 23 anonymous research participants who agreed to share with me some of their most private life experiences. Many said they never told anyone what they shared with me; I hope that you, the reader, learn a great deal from their experiences as I share them with their permission, throughout this book. You all were more candid with me than I anticipated, and generous with sharing your life experiences. Thank you so much for what you have shared; I hope that this book does your stories justice.

I am grateful to Oklahoma State University for awarding me a sabbatical to focus on writing this book; had I not had that time to focus on writing, this book would not have been completed. Thank you Dr. Lu Bailey for helpful advice about framing some of the issues in this book, and for showing what it means to be a spectacular colleague. I cherish our special connection as scholars who do our best to make a difference despite any circumstance. Thank you also to Dr. Jesse Mendez. You are the most supportive supervisor I have had in the last 2 decades; I am a far more productive scholar due to your support. I hope we can share a wall again someday!

There are many national organizations working to curb the ugly tide of pornography, which have in one way or another been helpful to me as I wrote this book. I'm indebted to people like Brandon Rietz, Ted Shimer, and Dave Riner from what I believe is the most fruitful ministry in the United States, Student Mobilization (www.stumo.org). Thank you to everyone with StuMo for all you do! Thank you also to Clay Olsen and Ryan Clark Werner and the great folks at *Fight the New Drug*. You were so generous in sharing materials with me about the Fortify Program! I am a big fan; thank you for the impact you are having and will continue to have on people who struggle worldwide. Thank you also to Patrick Trueman, Dawn Hawkins, and everyone at the National Center on Sexual Exploitation for featuring my research on your website and for taking such a strong leadership role in the fight against the sexually exploitive effects of pornography. I am honored to be part of your war on illegal pornography; I look forward to learning form the setbacks and rejoicing in the many victories ahead.

In my travels across the country to speak and train people about sexual violence prevention and the harms of pornography, I meet so many inspiring people who encourage my work. Though there are too many to mention in these pages, special thanks to Deb Crater, Gerald Longjohn, Steve Ivester, Allison Ash, Drew Boa, Drew Moser, Skip Trudeau, Ryan Hawkins, Mark Muha, Barb Cyr-Roman, Brad Cerasuolo, Todd Barriger, Scott Collard, Steve Beers, Brad Lau, Jessica Rimmer, Julie Elliot, and Dan Falk.

Several other people have sustained me on a personal and spiritual level as I have gone about the writing process. I feel a special debt of gratitude to people who have prayed for me throughout the writing process – thank you to all who prayed so fervently. Those prayers were felt as deeply and earnestly as I know they were offered. Dale, my mentor, brother, and friend; you consistently provided valuable insight and wisdom as I conceptualized many of the issues in this book. Thank you for your unwavering commitment to my growth. Thank you Brett for your unvarnished honesty, your commitment to our brotherhood in Christ, and for your metacognition. Thank you David, for sharing so much of your life with me and for the way we remain steadfast brothers. I love you and your family deeply. Thank you Jeremy for teaching me the value of accountability, for a deep commitment to our friendship, and for confronting me when I need it.

Thank you to the wonderful families of Barzel for reminding me how precious it is to live in community, and to the members of Faith Bible Church for their prayers, encouragement, and commitment to the Word. My loving wife, children, and mother have been incredibly patient with me throughout the writing of this book, sharing the joy as I finished each chapter, and making sacrifices that I wish were not necessary. I could not ask for a better wife, son, daughter, or mother. Though they likely will not read this book anytime soon, I am so thankful that God brought each of them into my life. Most of all,

I am indebted to Jesus my savior, in whom I find life and meaning; very special thanks to Josh McDowell for pushing me toward Him.

As with all of my work, this book is dedicated to the glory of God.

John D. Foubert, Ph.D.
Oklahoma City, OK

Cautionary Disclaimer

This book pulls no punches. My goal is to describe the activities of the pornography industry in an unvarnished way, while avoiding gratuitous, overly graphic descriptions of what they do. Balancing these extremes is difficult. I prefer to state matters plainly, and write for a discerning reader who is in a place to read difficult material. Parts of this book will be difficult to read, as it describes total depravity. People I interviewed for this book were sexually abused, at least two committed sexual abuse, and many have had gut wrenching life experiences. I want you to know their stories, if you feel ready to read them, so that you can understand the depths of harm done by the pornography industry to our world.

I have chosen descriptive, rather than profane language, to describe content. Still, what is described in some parts is not fit for pre-teens in my view, and might well startle many adults.

If you have experienced sexual violence or sexual abuse, find it very difficult to read about violence, or otherwise think you might be offended by what you read, I advise you to give this book to someone else instead of reading it yourself. Two organizations that can be helpful are RAINN and One in Six.

Descriptions of pornography are not intended to produce sexual arousal, and descriptions of some violent behavior are not written to condone it. Rather, these are included to introduce testimony to indict the pornography industry with committing and encouraging violence against the bodies, minds, and souls of today's youth and young adults.

I caution you to only read this book if you are ready to hear the reality of what is happening and want to be motivated to make a difference.

Chapter 1

Why You Should Care About Pornography

Not long ago, the total depravity of pornography struck me in the face and shocked my conscience. While researching ways to prevent sexual violence on college campuses I was struck by how the pornography industry undermined my work without mercy. I wrote this book with the intent of shocking your conscience as well. I want you to know why viewing pornography should be avoided, beyond many of the obvious reasons that may occur to you at the outset. I also want to motivate you to work to fight an industry that is bent on stealing the sex drive of every person they can, while they redirect it to be satisfied only through their products and services.

I want you to understand the very latest research, perspectives of people who study pornography, and the real life stories of those whose lives have been forever changed by the degeneracy of an industry that makes billions by hijacking the very part of a person God intended to bond them to a spouse – their sexuality. The intent of this book is to describe to teens, young adults, parents, and pastors what the best research today shows about the harms of pornography so that you will have a thorough understanding of the intent and effect of today's porn. We need a more well-informed public debate about the actual harms of pornography; I sought to distill the available research for you into this book so that you can have a better informed perspective on the real, devastating harms of pornography. You will read interviews from scholars, some Christian and some not, who have studied pornography for many years. You'll read interviews from dozens of people, some Christian some not, whose lives have been changed forever because of the lies they were sold by the porn industry. As a Christian, I write from that worldview; I also hope that people, regardless of their religious perspective, will find much to learn in these pages.

I often hear the argument that people who perform in pornographic media choose to be there, love what they do, and find it empowering. Reality exposes those perspectives, propagated by the porn industry, are lies.

> "It is degrading. You are constantly called names, you are constantly beat, choked, gagged; there are actually a lot of women who are held against their will. There was one girl I helped that was held against her will for about 4 days and was violently raped during that period. Yeah the producer, after a long series of legal back and forth, finally was prosecuted and sent to jail for a short period of time. But he didn't get the sentence he should have got. It is just crazy that someone can get away with such a violent act against someone but everybody justifies it because you know they say, 'Oh well, these women ask for it because this is the life that they chose.' It is anything but empowering."

These are the words of January Villarubia, who like most women who have been in the porn industry, went by an assumed name in her films. Alongside the latest research about porn, you will meet her, and many others whose lives have been affected by pornography, in this book.

As we explore these issues, I hope you will develop a deeper understanding of the true effects of pornography so that you can be in the best position possible to help friends, relatives, and others see the devastating reality of what the pornography industry is doing, and how we can fight back.

Porn is Violent

In the past few decades, violence in pornography has grown from a occurring in a small niche market, to being more common, to being in almost every scene and image.[1] [2] Pornography scholar Megan Tyler notes that the early 1990s brought in a new level of violence into mainstream pornography. In the late 1990s, violence increased further. Most recently, acts so violent that they lead women to vomit, are mainstream.[3] Scenes degrading women by showing men's bodily fluids on their face are now commonplace on the Internet.[4] Though some pornographers, and those who support them, occasionally play down the violence in pornography, scholars who study pornography note that men in the industry celebrate the fact that their work is abusive.[5]

Why do you need to know this if you don't already? For too long, people in the Christian community, and others, have thought of pornography as a private sin that shouldn't be discussed by the Church. That has fed a culture where the pornography use of many is relegated to unacknowledged sin, private shame, or hopeless losing battles. It is time for the Church, and indeed all people of conscience, to fight – armed with the truth, and strengthened by numbers.

One of the scholars I interviewed for this book, Dr. Robert Jensen, is a professor of journalism at the University of Texas and the author of

Getting Off: Pornography and the End of Masculinity.[6] Dr. Jensen has studied trends in pornography for several decades. He commented on the change in pornography in recent decades.

> "In the last 25 years we know that porn got more aggressive, porn got more extreme. The sexualization of male dominance over females intensified. That is unquestionably true. Nobody in the industry would argue that. It doesn't mean that every image they produced was like that. But the intensity of the images increased. We also know that porn got more culturally acceptable, not that everybody likes it, but it is part of mainstream culture in a way it wasn't before. That is the paradox of porn. You would think that something that got more cruel, more callous, more aggressive and more racist at the same time would not become more acceptable in the culture. That tells you something important. It tells you that pornographic values are in fact mainstream. In some sense a lot of that was predictable. What wasn't predictable I think, although in retrospect it should have been, is the degree to which younger women would embrace porn as a sign of liberation. That caught me by surprise."

Porn is Central in American Culture

So just how mainstream is porn today? One in four Internet searches are done to access pornography.[7] Among all ages of adults in the United States, 64 per cent of men and 42 per cent of women view pornography at least monthly.[8] Another study broke this down by age ranges. Among men 18-30 years old, 63% viewed pornography more than once per week, 79% viewed pornography at least monthly. Among 18-30 year old women, 19% viewed porn more than once a week, 34% viewed it at least monthly. Not surprisingly, with increasing age comes less viewing. Still, among 50-68 year olds, 49% of men and 5% of women view pornography at least once a month.[9] Despite the fact that it is illegal for them to access pornography, the average child sees Internet pornography for the first time at age 11.[10] [11] Scholars I interviewed for this book suggest that if a study was done today on the age boys first see porn, it would be under 10 years old.

The mainstream nature of pornography in society today is made possible by the universal *accessibility* of pornography through portable electronic devices. Smart phones have allowed Internet pornography use to increase dramatically.[12] Along with accessibility, technological changes have made obtaining and viewing pornography something that people, regardless of their age, can do *anonymously*. In the past, to obtain pornography, people needed to interact directly with a live person – workers at video rental stores or checkout staff in convenience stores. Today, any teenager with a smart phone can access millions of free images through a simple web browser or specialized app. Rounding out the "Three A's" of pornography, *affordability* is another reason that use is so ubiquitous.[13] There is a lot of free porn available, even on the initial screens of paid websites.

Pornography is mainstream not only in popular culture, but also in the business world. In order to understand pornography, the first thing to realize is that it is a business that wants to maximize profit. In 2010, worldwide pornography revenues from a variety of sources (the Internet, sex shops, videos rented in hotel rooms) were approximately $100 billion.[14] That staggering amount of money is more than the combined revenues of Microsoft, Google, Amazon, eBay, Yahoo, Apple, and Netflix that same year.[15] The money that porn makes in the United States each year, about $13 billion, exceed the combined revenues of the National Football League, Major League Baseball, and the National Basketball Association.[16]

John D. Foubert, Ph.D.

When you think about where all of this money goes, you are likely thinking the big pornography producers. And to a large extent, you are right. However, a significant amount of money is also being made by companies that aren't usually thought of as being part of the larger money- generating machine of porn. Not long ago, Time Warner reportedly made so much money off of pornography that it had the rapt attention of their then CEO, Glenn Britt. In an article for a pornography business trade publication, Britt is quoted as complaining that revenues from their video on demand service were falling. He blamed the decline in profits on the rising availability of free online pornography.[17] Of course the major credit card companies make a lot of money from paid online sites. Many hotel chains make millions of dollars from pay-per-view porn in their rooms; though the number of chains who still offer in-room pornography is declining. There are many mainstream businesses that have a substantial investment in keeping pornography as a vibrant money-maker for them.

Of course, most pornography today is free to the user, at least at first. But people who use it for free still make money for the pornography websites through advertising revenue. The more people who visit a "free" porn site, the more money they can charge for advertising. Even free porn isn't really free. Another scholar I interviewed, Dr. Walter DeKeseredy, has written about 20 books and is the author of a prominent theory about sexual violence. Currently, he serves as Director of the Research Center on Violence at West Virginia University. According to Dr. DeKeseredy,

> "Why is so much porn free? Because they try to get you in other ways. You have all these ads when you go to these sites. Free pornography online is used to lure you into doing phone sex and to paying for watching. When you click on a movie, you often hear noise in the background, and there will be

a woman on live cams talking to you. That costs money ... It is all about money. I'm worried about how generations have been rewired. What is going to happen with people who have grown up on all this stuff? What worries me is that today's porn, of course there are different types, but a healthy portion of it is racist and violent. And how people are interacting with each other sexually is becoming more hurtful, and that hurtfulness is becoming more normative, and the average age that young men in the United States are watching these things is 11 years of age. Now it is really intense, crude, guttural, hateful, vicious stuff and people are consuming this so regularly. And so, how is this going to impact long term on our societal gender relations, that is what worries me."

If you were alive and old enough to understand the news in the year 1994, you likely remember the iconic picture of leaders of several big tobacco companies testifying before Congress.[18] In contrast to a mountain of data available, some of which they themselves reportedly suppressed, the tobacco industry executives testified that they didn't believe cigarettes were addictive. Interestingly, they also said they hoped that their own children wouldn't smoke. In a similar way, there are powerful voices today that try to convince the public that using pornography isn't harmful.[19] Their claims stand against well over 100 studies demonstrating that pornography harms people, often badly.[20][21] Just because someone who is powerful says something that sounds convincing, it doesn't make it accurate. Sometimes the motives are ulterior. As you read this book, I hope you won't trust the voices of the powerful so much as you will consider the evidence.

Pornography Impacts Behavior

Does viewing pornography impact people's behavior? The weight of the scientific evidence offers a convincing response: yes. How? Pornography creates a sexual script that then guides people's sexual experiences.[22] A sexual script is essentially the ideas that people have in their mind about how a sexual encounter unfolds from beginning to end. The script that today's pornography encourages is anything but loving, let alone honoring to God. It is extremely violent, steering people into selfish acts of sexualized violence. Pornography depicts a violent corruption of God's design for sexual relations between husband and wife.

Pornography scholar Pamela Paul notes that the ubiquity of pornography has made our culture "pornified," meaning that aspects of and values within pornography have seeped into popular culture. Indeed, the vast *majority* of movies made today are pornographic. The most recent data reveals that 11,000 new porn films are shot each year versus just 400 G, PG, PG-13, and R rated Hollywood movies. The 11,000 figure doesn't even include pornography that is not in a movie, such as in still photographs or increasingly popular short snippets on a website.[23]

Much of this book will detail the many ways that pornography impacts people's behavior. One such way is in sexual practices. In contrast to a Biblical model for sexual relations, much of today's pornography includes male to female anal sex. There is growing evidence that men are requesting this behavior in their own sexual relationships. In my interview with Dr. DeKeseredy, he noted "When I read the medical journals, I notice that we are seeing a substantial increase in rectal damage of women because anal sex is an integral part of today's pornography" and these activities are being mimicked in actual encounters. He continued, "there are a lot of medical issues there."

Perhaps more than any group, pornography is impacting young men. One of the leading scholars of gender and masculinity is Dr. Michael Kimmel, a professor at SUNY Stony Brook. He describes a typical pornography scene as an "erotic paradise where both women and men are constantly on the prowl, looking for opportunities for sexual gratification ... the pornographic fantasy is a fantasy where women's sexuality is not their own, but is in fact a projection of men's sexuality"[24] (p. 173, Kimmel, 2008).

No wonder so many guys want to look, and get hooked. One of Kimmel's more interesting findings is that young men gravitate toward more extreme, violent forms of pornography. Their viewing patterns are often group oriented with casual banter among guys making fun of the women in the images they ingest. By contrast, today's adult men tend to watch pornography alone or with a partner, and lean toward genres where women appear to have high sexual desire and enjoy what they are doing. Younger guys do not typically seek women's expressed pleasure in pornographic media. Though the female actor may speak words of enjoyment, the facial expressions, tears, and positions make the woman out to be pained, prostituted, and humiliated. Furthermore, the language used by pornography users encourages the denigration of women.[25]

Another harm, referred to in my interview with Dr. Robert Jensen, comes up in men's intimate relationships.

> "On the male side, more and more men will say that their own use of pornography, especially those who use it habitually, it has an effect on their ability to be intimate with female partners. I don't know how many times I've heard men say 'I can't get an erection without thinking about porn. I can't perform sexually if I don't' have a pornographic loop going on in my mind.' That is not the speculation

of 'crazy radical feminists,' that is the self-reports of lots of men."

One of the leading thinkers about pornography today is philosopher Dr. Rebecca Whisnant at the University of Dayton. When I interviewed Dr. Whisnant, she noted that

> "For men, in particular, this is an industry that is invested in getting you hooked early on a certain way of experiencing your sexuality and getting you dependent on corporate produced images to experience yourself as a sexual being, to filter your perceptions of the people you might like to be sexual with. And they want to do that because it makes them money."

Another scholar I will introduce you to in this book is Dr. Mary Anne Layden; she is the Director of the Sexual Trauma and Psychopathology Program at the University of Pennsylvania. She points to yet another harm of pornography she realized through her practice as a therapist. In a book chapter she wrote in *The Social Costs of Pornography* she shared

> "I've been a psychotherapist for 25 years. I specialize in the treatment of sexual violence victims and perpetrators and sex addicts. I spend all day, every day talking to rapists, and rape victims, pedophiles and incest survivors, sex addicts, pornography addicts, prostitutes, strippers, and pornography models. After I had done this work for about 10 years, I had a sudden realization that I hadn't treated one case of sexual violence that didn't involve pornography. You don't have to have a Ph.D. in psychology to realize something is going on here."[26]

The people she has treated evidence the link between pornography and sexual violence. We will go into this phenomenon in detail in chapter four.

Indeed, something is going on here. In the rest of the book, we will explore all of these issues thoroughly. As we do, the definition I will use for pornography is one used by Christian researcher Michael Lastoria, "Any kind of material aimed at creating or enhancing sexual feelings or thoughts in the recipient and at the same time containing explicit exposure and/or descriptions of the genitals and/or sexual acts."[27] This definition encompasses pornographic materials such as videos, pictures, and text. This definition will allow us to look broadly at a wide variety of impacts. The research on these impacts sends a strong message: pornography inflicts devastating harms on the viewer.

Why This Book

I wrote this book so that Christians could gain a better understanding of the research on how pornography is harming our relationships, our society, and us. I also hope that is proves useful to a wider audience. Depending upon how you view the world, you may believe that pornography harms a great deal or little to not at all. You may believe that there are some obvious benefits to pornography. I start by saying I respect where you, the reader, are coming from on this topic. What I hope you will consider as you read this book is that there are harms of pornography that you likely have not thought about before. Whether you think porn is a cancer on the souls in our society or is a tool for women's empowerment, I hope that you will read this book critically and consider the evidence it offers.

I wrote this book to shock your conscience because shocked consciences promote action – and action is exactly what I hope to inspire. Action to curtail the use of pornography, action to protect our children from having their sexuality hijacked, and action to hold pornographer's accountable for their distribution of illegal, obscene material. I don't intend to make my arguments with flimsy statistics or hyperbolic statements. Rather, I intend to expose you to the reality of the content, intent, and effects of pornography on you and those you love. It may be that you have viewed pornography a few times and thought it was gross, you may love it and watch it daily, you may have never seen it. No matter what exposure to pornography you have had, others around you have been exposed. The statistics I share in this chapter, and throughout the book, testify to that reality. Pornography use has become nearly ubiquitous for men in the United States, for a growing number of women, and for a majority of teens. The lessons they learn from porn shape our culture – the culture you inhabit.

I intend to describe in the plainest and most reliable way possible, the effects of pornography. I am a scholar who has studied and written about sexual violence since 1992; I've studied pornography since about 2006. In addition to findings from rigorous, peer-reviewed research, I will interweave the life stories of people like you and those you know. They will describe how pornography has affected their lives. Their stories are likely to resonate with you. Each research participant I interviewed selected their own pseudonym for this book, so I will refer to each using the name they chose. I will also share a few things that will help you understand them as real people with real stories. Some of them follow Jesus; others do not. In many cases, I have altered small details that are not central to understanding their lives, in order to help protect their anonymity. I also took the liberty of editing out extraneous phrases they used that don't add meaning to what they described. I have printed some of their vernacular, so that the reader can get a sense of them as real people. In this book, I will also share the perspectives of some of the most renowned scholars and thought leaders about pornography today. Their real names are used, with their permission. This book will introduce you to their professional roles and their best research and ideas about pornography.

I caution you. If you are someone who has experienced sexual violence or someone who might be described as "easily grossed out" – there are portions of this book that you may find very difficult to read. You may choose not to read some parts or even choose not to read this book at all and give it away to a friend. While doing the research for this book, I often became sick to my stomach or deeply disturbed by the research I read, and the interviews I conducted. I encourage you to proceed cautiously with reading what is contained in this book. Do so if and only if you believe you are ready to hear that which is disturbing. And please take good care of yourself as you do. My great hope is that this book will play a pivotal role in motivating a new generation of people who can speak intelligently about the harms of pornography and why we need to band together to fight the hundred billion dollar porn industry. The health of the next generation depends upon it. Thank you for choosing this book. I hope you find it powerful, informative, and motivating. To hear me speak about each chapter and for updated statistics as they come out, please visit my website, www.johnfoubert.com. I will update these thoughts regularly to provide the latest information possible.

Chapter 2

A Christian Perspective on Pornography

This chapter reviews what the Bible has to say about pornography, along with personal anecdotes and research that speaks to the intersection between pornography and religiosity. Obviously computers weren't around in Biblical times; however, there are several Biblical principles with clear ties to the use and making of pornography. Though the aim of this book is not to be a comprehensive exploration of scripture and pornography, in order to frame a context for the data shared in this book, a review of Biblical teaching about pornography is useful. Moreover, I will review first person anecdotes, scholarly interviews, and published studies connecting pornography and Christian teaching.

In the interviews I conducted for this book, I was struck by how frequently and passionately the research participants I spoke with – who came from many different religious and nonreligious traditions -- brought up their religious or spiritual beliefs. This chapter will offer you an unvarnished look into their perspectives and particularly how their faith informs them. I will also explore some of available research that speaks to the connection between pornography and spiritual beliefs, including research I recently completed.

Biblical Perspective

To explore what the Bible has to say about pornography, I interviewed Dr. Mark Hitchcock, an adjunct professor at Dallas Theological Seminary and author of 20 books including *The End: A Complete Overview of Bible Prophecy and the End of Days.*[28] He noted passages in Genesis that showed God's high regard for monogamous relationships between one man and one woman in marriage; those relationships are set apart as holy. Dr. Hitchcock stated,

> "What pornography does is it tears away at the seams of the one flesh, monogamous, heterosexual relationship, because it brings another party into that … and anything that destroys that or tears away at that is harmful to the individuals, harmful to the family, and then, ultimately, to society." He continued, "And then you get in the New Testament with Jesus teaching that if you look on a woman and lust after her you've committed adultery in your heart. Well, you can't really look at pornography without that [lust] happening … and so, you don't have to be a Bible scholar to understand that it is something that God forbids."

Dr. Hitchcock also noted that in Paul's New Testament letters, the topic of pornography comes up.

> "It's 'pornea' – it is just a broad term for sexual sins, sexual behavior, obviously prostitution; pornography comes from that, the word 'prostitute.' That is why I think Jesus says don't divorce your wife except for pornea; he doesn't say adultery! I think there are valid reasons to get divorced [besides] adultery. I think if a woman is married to a man who is

addicted to pornography and he won't quit, I mean, he won't repent of it; that destroys a person, it eats away the fiber of their heart and their soul. So I think that God uses that broad term."

Though viewing pornographic images is not a struggle for him, Dr. Hitchcock described a time when he was 10 years old and a friend showed him pornography.

"I had a friend of mine who had an older brother, and his brother's room was next to his, and he would go in there one time and say, 'Hey man, look at these magazines I found from my brother!' Well, I looked at that stuff when I was a kid and it had a really bad effect on me. And I felt guilty about it; I didn't know why. I mean, nobody ever told me anything about that and I didn't tell my parents about it because I didn't know what to think. I really think that had a bad effect on my life. I never had a problem with pornography after that; it wasn't that that sunk me into some problem ... I do think as a young person, I've thought about this a lot, that in some way that it did create in me a little bit, maybe an objectifying of women. I felt later it was something I had to deal with in life that I didn't have the connection or compassion because we looked at that a decent amount [at age 10], my friend and I did, and then I realized this is not good, it is bad, it makes me feel bad."

Students at Christian Colleges

Using a broad definition of pornography, that of viewing nudity or sexual images on the Internet, a Christian research team led by

Dr. Michael Lastoria of Houghton College found in a nationwide survey of students who attend Christian colleges that pornography use is common. Among male students, 14% viewed pornography monthly, an additional 20% viewed it at least weekly, and 5% more viewed it at least daily. Only 14% never saw pornography. Women on these campuses were far different than the men. Only 3% viewed pornography monthly or more, 80% never saw it. The level of use by women at Christian colleges is far lower than women in the general public.[29]

When Dr. Lastoria analyzed the data on students at Christian colleges, he found that the more students reported that their life was influenced by their religious beliefs, the less they viewed pornography. This result is part of a pattern of findings we will explore throughout the remainder of this chapter – the more people view their religious beliefs as important to them, and important enough to act upon, the less they watch pornography. In Lastoria's study, students who cognitively bought in to the mission and culture of their institution were more likely to have their behavior be consistent with that mission. A later study confirmed the finding that internalized religious beliefs go along with less pornography use.[30] Related research shows that the more men at evangelical Christian colleges access Internet pornography, the more guilt they experience about their use. In addition, men attending these colleges who do not personally identify as evangelical, look at pornography more hours each week than evangelical men.[31]

How Deep is The Belief?

Building on the research mentioned above, I conducted a study along with my colleague Andrew Rizzo, looking at pornography use among students at a public university. We explored the relationships between two different kinds of approaches to religion. First, we looked at people with religious practices that were motivated out of self-centered motives (extrinsic). These include participating in religious activities to increase social standing or participating in prayer in order to be happy. Conversely, we looked at those with religious practices anchored in a desire to live out one's faith, read the sacred texts of one's religion, and a desire to have one's beliefs and behavior match (intrinsic). We found that the more men were motivated to be religious because it could help their social standing, the more they also used pornography. The more men and women were motivated to be religious for selfless reasons, desiring to have ones beliefs and behavior match, the less they viewed pornography.[32] An even more recent study has very similar findings; both men and women who are religious for selfless reasons are also less likely to use pornography.[33]

Struggles With Pornography

Christian men who I interviewed for this book often described an active struggle with their pornography use, at least at different times of their lives. Greg noted that his pornography use conflicted with his beliefs as a Christian.

> "The person I tried to and said I tried to model my life after [Jesus] said that if you are looking at a woman with lust, it is like you are committing adultery with her. In my mind I'm already damaged goods, like wow, how many times have I done that! It was a dual life. On one side I'm the Christian school kid with all the answers who, like, leads worship, who knocks all the questions out of the park in youth group discussion, yet here I have cultivated this habit my whole life. I was depressed often and I think pornography is intimately involved with that somehow."

Tommy noted how he would stop using pornography when he got more into his Catholic faith, yet would start using again when a spiritual high wore off. He said,

> "I spoke at church camps, whenever I came back from them it was always, like, easy to keep away from it for a time period, because I felt renewed, every time it was a life changing experience. Like they had church everyday and like confession and a bunch of lessons and stuff and it became just apparent that I didn't need that [pornography]. I didn't want that and you go back home in the real world and you sink into society again. A few weeks later you just get back into it." He continued, "I think as far as the negative side goes with it, like, Pope John Paul II had a quote, 'Pornography is not bad because it shows too much, but that it shows too little of a person.' I kinda thought about that and it is kinda true. Kinda looking at someone in a way that God doesn't tell you to look at someone. And you are not looking at them for who they are but what they look like. But I don't think it will ever, like, go away, because it is, like, human nature. I don't think it is necessarily wrong to look at it and masturbate because you have that hormone, that desire to look at it."

Clearly, there are ways in which Tommy's faith helped him stay away from pornography; yet, he does not fully embrace a Biblical worldview, given his reasoning that it isn't wrong to look at pornography because he has hormones.

Addiction

Much is said inside and outside Christian circles about whether pornography can be addictive. Most people and scholarly sources I came across argue that it can be and often is.[34] In my interview with Dr. Hitchcock, he noted,

> "I think some people are more prone to addictive behavior than other people are … if you don't know who has that [an addictive personality] and the first time or first few times they look at it, it sets this thing off in your brain. Some people have that and they don't know they have it until they are hooked. That is why you try to keep people away. I don't think you could ever keep a young man away from seeing that now. I think it is impossible. Cause everyone has that curiosity at least one time just to look."

Dr. Hitchcock continued,

> "This has got the power to totally overtake someone's life like cocaine or heroin. When you get into any sin you are opening up a bunch of potential consequences and you don't really know what they are going to be. You could get addicted, it could really mess your wife up, it could mess you up, it could make you not desire your wife any more, it can diminish your sexual satisfaction with your wife, I mean and you don't know maybe none of those things will happen or something will. This [pornography use] is not right, and when you do it, you will sense that it is not right. No one will have to tell you. You'll know it is wrong when you are doing it cause you are going to sneak around when you do it. And if somebody walked in, you are not

going to want [that person] to see you doing that, so you are going to know it is wrong. The first thing I tell people with anything like that is the reason you don't want to do this is because it has a bad effect on your relationship with God and that is the most important thing in the world ... And so, that is the real issue, it is going to stunt relationship with God and when your relationship with God is not what it should be, everything is going to be affected."

This realization that using pornography affects one's relationship with God is something that Ella, an African American woman in her 20s, began to understand after she started looking at pornography. She related,

"Moving closer to God, I realized that it [pornography] is not something to be played with. It is an addiction that can start so innocently and spin outward. It wasn't something that I thought of as a God thing at first; I just felt it and then I realized how bad I felt and then when I would read the Bible or go to church and my pastor would talk about how he was addicted to porn. It just opened up this world. So, I was like, 'Wow, just like alcoholism, just like being addicted to cocaine, it is a serious issue for a lot of people and you have to have God on your side to battle it.'"

Similarly, Bob, a Native American 21-year-old college student, noted that pornography affected his relationship with God. "Yes, I just know it is bad. Obviously these women are the daughters of God and you aren't supposed to look at them that way, that is why I want to stop but I keep, like, going back." When I asked Bob why he didn't stop using pornography, he stated, "I think it is an addiction kind of. I kinda use it as a stress relief and that is why I go back." I asked him if he found a better stress reliever would he be more likely to not use pornography. He said yes.

Herein lies part of a potential strategy for people who want to stop using pornography. One should figure out why they are using it and develop a healthy habit to replace it. Of course, it isn't good to replace one addiction with another. Yet, one of the best pieces of advice I heard in the interviews I conducted with scholars was from Dr. Hitchcock. He noted that a vibrant spiritual life – reading the Bible, spending time with God's people, practicing the spiritual disciplines – is the best way to prevent, and come out of, an addiction.

A Swat Team and a Jail Cell

For some men, it takes serious consequences to give up pornography. For Joe, it took a six-month jail sentence. Joe is nearly 70 years old, is a member of a Mainline Protestant denomination, and was arrested for possession and distribution of child pornography. I share most of his story in a later chapter. When I interviewed Joe, he described years of downloading and then sharing pictures of girls through his computer. Obviously, and he admits, this is a more serious matter than looking at adult pornography. The consequences of Joe's actions caught up with him. He described his first night in jail.

> "Man, that night, I just laid there, just what in the world has happened to me, good God I thought I was a Christian, God why have you forsaken me? [He laughed nervously]. Then I realized it wasn't God who had forsaken me; I had forsaken God. I was almost arrogant about that, [thinking before I was arrested that] 'God loves me so much that he don't care what I been doing.' Well, he showed me how much he cared. But I'm really glad that He did

care enough for me; that He give me that chance to redeem myself." He continued, "When they first arrested me [by storming his house in the middle of the night, guns drawn], I was in jail only 3 or 4 days. I was so devastated when they put me in there, those guys [police] were telling me that I was going to get at least 10 years, and my wife was wanting to hire an attorney for me. And I had already decided that I wasn't going to do 10 years in jail. I'm old, 10 years is a life sentence, I just figured I was going to die in jail anyway. I decided to kill myself."

Joe didn't kill himself. He stopped all viewing of pornography. He spent several months in jail. He told me that getting caught was

"probably the best thing that ever happened to me because being free of this pornography is like finding Jesus all over again … I had never completely turned my life over to Him, I always felt like I was holding back some. I guarantee when I was sitting in that jailhouse that night I turned it over to Him. I don't have that feeling that I'm holding back on Him anymore. I used to think that, 'Man, it would be great if I could just completely turn my life over to Christ' but I didn't feel like I had ever really done that. Like I said, I prayed the prayer and thought I was saved, but I don't think I really was."

Indeed, his use of child pornography is something most people would agree was not only illegal, but morally abhorrent. In time, he came to agree with this perception. Interestingly, part of his coming to understand that what he was doing was wrong involved a change in his religious perspective, from being more selfish to selfless. He described a moment in jail when he was hitting rock bottom. He was very sick and was unable to receive treatment, staying in an overcrowded jail cell with people who wanted to hurt him. He cried out,

> "I was praying 'Lord I am doing everything I know to get out of this, there is nobody in this jail who prays any more or who is trying harder to be who you want them to be than I am!' But he told me, 'Joe, this is just a sample of what I went through for you.'"

This marked a turning point for Joe, realizing the grace of God, and deciding to follow him for more intrinsic rather than extrinsic reasons.

Overcoming Addiction and Other Problematic Use

I asked Joe what might have stopped him from looking at pornography before he was arrested. He said,

> "I don't know what would have reached me. One of my big fears was that [my wife] was going to tell the preacher that I was looking at pornography. I'm tempted to tell wives to tell the preacher if their husbands are looking at pornography. I also have a support group and I ask the guys to hold me accountable, and that is a great thing to have is someone to hold you accountable. That is one way you keep from reoffending."

Greg, a man who identifies as Christian and has been addicted to pornography for at least 10 years, noted how talking with other Christians was helpful to him in his ongoing recovery.

"I had a friend who shared my religious beliefs, who confessed to me that he had struggled with sexual issues like that [pornography] and he had overcome them and he was a different person. I was very interested and I kept asking him about it and he told me he was involved in this Christian counseling program ministry called Pure Life Ministries in Kentucky, this 'overcomers at home' thing. I was broken at that point where I saw how helpless I was and for the first time I was willing to do what it took to actually follow Christ and get free of this. So, I enrolled in that program, they were having me read the Bible every day and they were having me pray for other people every day instead of myself. I'd pray for other people, friends, family, anyone else. The idea is that addicts and people like that are pretty self-absorbed. Praying for others helps you be not self-absorbed. There is a spiritual element to that too."

I asked Dr. Hitchcock what he recommends to people who want to either avoid or stop using pornography. He said,

"I would also tell young people, too, when it comes to sins of the flesh, there is the world, the flesh, and the devil. And the Bible tells us how to deal with each of those kinds of sin. With sins of the flesh, the Bible is consistent always in what it says – flee! Flee youthful lust, flee sexual immorality. You know, Joseph fleeing. It is never stand and fight. When it comes to Satanic opposition it says, having done everything stand, stand firm, stand against the wiles of the devil, it is always hold your ground, stand. When it comes to the sins of the flesh, it never says stand. It says run! You turn that computer on, I'm going to look at this, now I'm going to stand. Well no you are not, man, you're going down; you have to flee!"

If someone is addicted, Dr. Hitchcock suggests,

"if I had someone come in who was addicted to pornography, I would meet with them first a bit. I think the ultimate answer to that is a vibrant spiritual life, because if you have a vibrant spiritual life that is what is going to allow you to overcome [the addiction]. Just gritting your teeth and trying harder if you are in the clutches of that [won't work], you have got to fill that with something else. You have got to want to be pure, 'I want to live the way God wants me to live so I am going to do the spiritual disciplines of reading the Bible and prayer and spending time with my wife and all these different things.' And then asking God as you are growing spiritually for that desire to diminish and for Him to give you the strength to flee from it."

Paul, a college student who follows Jesus, mentioned that his pornography addiction had a huge effect on his relationship with God.

"At first I knew it was wrong, but I did it anyways and masturbation came along with that and then after being constantly convicted by God, Himself, and Him pursuing me on a constant basis through it, I got to a point where I was just, I was so captivated by porn and I wanted to get away from it. I couldn't myself; I had come to a point where I just felt like I didn't have any control over myself. I would know taking the phone into the bathroom that I would be looking at porn and masturbating and I didn't want to, but I did and afterward I would just feel worse. I would know that this is affecting my relationship with God, this is affecting future relationships with women that I'm going to have, but I did it anyways. So, I came to a point where I started talking to my Dad about it and reading through books by a man named Joshua Harris called 'Sex is not the problem, Lust is.' But through Dad holding me accountable, putting passwords on my iTouch and iPhone, getting different browsers like X3watch, and stuff like that to hold me accountable was huge. Also, after coming to a point where I realized I really have to give up this habitual sin to Christ, it talks about it in Philippians 10 of how strongholds and thresholds that have a hold of you, you have to give up to Christ completely. At first I didn't really understand, so how in the world am I supposed to put this on someone else? But through learning more and more about my relationship with Jesus and God and growing and learning about who Jesus is and what His purpose on this earth is, and all kind of spiritual growth, it became easier to just let go of it. I still struggle with lust and pornography and it is a daily battle but I know that I'm not in it alone. I've got my accountability partners and I've got Jesus Christ and again just going back to my growth and relationship with Him has helped because instead of spending so much time looking at porn. It took years to get where I am at now. Just like daily devotionals and quiet times and times in prayer and when I would be tempted, of course, just to call on Him. A big thing for me is Bible verse memorization. It is a big avenue for me because when I am tempted or feel like I have the urges to find some way to look at porn, or like that lustful or lusting after someone, I start to, like, recite verses that I memorized. That would get my mind off it and that has been a huge escape for me. Coming out of it has helped my relationship grow over the long haul and I understand that I will have consequences, even though I am forgiven. But I do know that … I am forgiven and Jesus Christ loves me no matter what and I can go from there." Paul has gone two years without looking at pornography.

Greg had similar thoughts on fighting an addiction.

"I'd say accountability is one of the main weapons for me; faith is the main weapon. My true self is resurrected in Christ. I see now Christ wins. The old me doesn't win, pornography doesn't win, which gives me hope in the fight against addiction and in life in general."

I asked Dr. Hitchcock what advice he gives to parents about protecting their children from pornography. He mentioned what he did in his own family.

"I've talked to my wife about that stuff … I think [it] is important for husbands to help educate their wives about it. There is also a relational element to this, for people who are married, where the husband and wife really need to work together. If you are married, you are one, and it really is a problem for both of you. And the husband needs to educate his wife about it and he needs to help educate the wife about their sons. I just told [my wife] about it, be observant if they are in ... [their] room a lot on their computer, or whatever, just know that they may not be looking at a video game."

Concluding Thought

From the research and viewpoints gathered for this chapter, several themes come up. First, people who are more devout tend to use pornography less. In fact, research on adolescents shows that the more religious they are, the less intentional and accidental exposure they have to pornography.[35] Second, connecting with a faith community and living out one's faith can be helpful in overcoming problematic use of pornography. Finally, when people do sink more deeply into pornography, many describe that as an experience that harms their religious or spiritual side.

Chapter 3

Porn and the Brain

You may have heard that pornography rewires the brain. Or that it causes erectile dysfunction. Or that it is addictive. There is strong evidence to support all of these conclusions. [36] In this chapter, I invite you to join me as we explore pornography's biological effects.

Porn Rewires the Brain

In recent years, one of the most interesting findings about the effects of pornography focuses on how pornographic images rewire the brain. Gaining an understanding of exactly how the brain can be rewired is important in order to have a full understanding of how viewing pornography can impact the behavior of those you love.

In an article about pornography and the male brain, Dr. William Struthers, author of *Wired for Intimacy: How Pornography Hijacks the Male Brian*, noted,

> "The on-demand availability of robust sexual stimuli presents a unique problem for developing and maintaining a healthy sexuality. The ease of access, variety of images, and the vigorous sensory constitution of this media go beyond the strength

of mental imagery and fantasy. People can see whatever they want, whenever they want, however they want. In doing so they can generate, serve, and satisfy their sensual nature. Pornography creates a world today where the consumer (usually men) has the ability to bring up at their whim graphic (and sometimes interactive) depictions of nudity and sexual encounters. Women are perpetually available for their pleasure with minimal immediate consequences. People become disposable."[37]

Some of the most powerful studies of the brain and pornography come from investigating brain scans. In one experiment, the brains of men were scanned while they viewed porn. When neurologists looked at their brain imaging scans, men's brains reacted to women as if they were objects, not people.[38] This is important because it is the process of dehumanizing a person that makes violence against them much more acceptable.[39]

Research comparing the brains of people who are addicted to pornography versus those who are not has found that addicts *like* pornography just as much as others, but they *desire* it much more. So, when brain scans of men who are addicted to pornography are compared to non-addicts, they both respond the same way in their "liking centers" but respond differently in the "desire centers" of their brains. When addicted men were shown pornography while their brains were being scanned, their dorsal anterior cingulate, ventral striatum and amygdala were activated – showing a strong desire for the material, more so than other, non-addicted men. In short, all men tested liked pornography, addicted men felt like they had to have it.[40] In an interesting twist, the men who were addicted to pornography had first seen porn much earlier in their lives than did the healthy men.

Gary Wilson has conducted a series of studies about pornography and the brain. Wilson is the author of the book *Your Brain on Porn*[41] and the website of the same name. His research supports the conclusion that pornography retrains the brain. He found that the very maps that nerve cells travel through the brain become re-routed as people use more and more pornography. A main point to remember is "nerve cells that fire together, wire together" (Wilson, 2014, p. 68).

But how does this happen? If a person experiences sexual release through self-stimulation while watching pornography, their sexual desire becomes retrained from the pre-wired, God designed desire for sexual gratification achieved through interacting with another person, to the rewired desire for images on a screen. Furthermore, as men become less aroused by initial, more tame, images, they begin to seek novelty – often more violent images – to obtain the same level of physical and psychological arousal. This "novelty and habituation" effect has been shown experimentally. Specifically, men were shown the same explicit film repeatedly. After time, they found it less arousing (they habituated to it), but once exposed to a new film (novelty) their arousal increased to the same level as it was when first seeing the initial film. In short, the same old images become boring after awhile, so the body seeks new ones to keep its arousal up.[42]

This habituation rang true with Greg, a research participant for this book. Greg is a secondary school teacher in a private school and part-time graduate student who is about to turn 30. He comes across as charismatic, good looking, and thoughtful. Greg is a devout follower of Jesus. He also admits to a lifelong battle, indeed addiction, to pornography. He described some of his initial forays into pornography like this:

> "At first watching people have sex disturbed me, I
> didn't want to see it. But then slowly, it is totally

a drug. I developed *tolerance. So what shocked me became interesting and what used to interest me became boring. And it took more variety, more frequency to get the same effect.* And the really wicked part about it is it gets more perverted. So I felt that happening and it terrified me. After a while I realized I was addicted and I needed to do anything it takes to get out of this."

Greg is describing the rewiring of his brain. Much of this rewiring occurs because of a brain chemical called dopamine. As Wilson describes it, dopamine functions within the body to motivate you to do what is in the best interest of your genes. The more dopamine that is released in your body, the more you are drawn to a particular experience. The highest amount of dopamine is released when someone is sexually stimulated and experiences sexual release. Other researchers have described dopamine as essentially the glue that holds together the connection of nerves in our brain that lead us to repeat behaviors.[43]

We learn from neuroscience that dopamine works alongside opioids. Dopamine influences the desire for an experience; the opioid makes you like it. Internet porn provides unlimited sexual stimuli, stimulating dopamine to continuously release to a chemical level that is nearly impossible to match through natural human bodily experiences. Thus the brain becomes trained for a level of stimulation (to quickly and constantly available computer images) that can't possibly be duplicated in real life.

When brain cells that fire together wire together,[44] the brain is linking up the nerves for sexual excitement with the nerves that store memories of how the body got to that level of excitement. When a viewer opens up a porn site that is found satisfying, the dopamine level in the brain and connections between nerve cells bond in stronger and stronger ways.

In the process of using more and more pornography, the brain gets used to self-stimulation to porn and feeling a pleasurable release. What people don't usually realize is that gradually, their brain starts to fight them. Professor Wilson found that when the brain keeps experiencing abnormally high levels of stimulation (such as with sexual release while watching porn), it moves into a protective mode of lowering the dopamine release, so that people will want less of the overly stimulating experience. So with less dopamine, the viewer becomes less satisfied with self-stimulating to the same old porn. The individual is then compelled to desperately seek stimulation that might elicit the same levels of a dopamine experienced previously. The brain changes, physically, and becomes desensitized to the images it saw before and needs more and more to reach the same levels of arousal. Just like the experience Greg just described. This greater need for stimulation is called tolerance. And tolerance is one of the key markers of addiction.

The process of rewiring the brain is also described by Dr. Struthers. The assertion that men are visual when it comes to sexuality is so commonly stated; few would argue that it has not made it into the everyday human vernacular. Noting this visual sensitivity, Dr. Struthers observed,

> "The male brain seems to be built in such a way that visual cues that have sexual relevance (e.g., the naked female form, solicitous facial expressions) have a hypnotic effect on him. When these cues are detected, they trigger a cascade of neurological, chemical, and hormonal events. In some ways they are like the "hit" of a drug—there is a rush of sexual arousal and energy that accompanies it. How a

man learns to deal with this energy and to form an appropriate response to it is part of becoming a mature adult. The psychological, behavioral, and emotional habits that form our sexual character will be based on the decisions we make. Whenever the sequence of arousal and response is activated, it forms a neurological memory that will influence future processing and response to sexual cues. As this pathway becomes activated and traveled, it becomes a preferred route—a mental journey—that is regularly trod. The consequences of this are far-reaching."[45]

Erectile Dysfunction

This rewiring of the brain leads to several other ill effects. The most disturbing to many men is erectile dysfunction, specifically, the inability to obtain and maintain an erection. Many men who become addicted to pornography experience both erectile dysfunction and decreased attraction to live partners. In fact over half of porn addicts have one or the other of these two experiences.[46] Building on this research, another set of neurologists found that if a man's use of porn is 'compulsive,' there is a greater than 50% chance he will have difficulty achieving an erection with a real partner, but will have no trouble having erections with porn.[47]

These effects are a major concern Greg reported. He said,

> "Based on my experience with it, it is an addiction, I know that dopamine is involved, neural pathways are involved. I have trained myself over the years through the use of pornography. I've just basically reversed the dopamine in my brain; my natural functions have rerouted. So I think that sex with a

real person who would be my wife wouldn't work like it should if I ever get married. Like it may not be stimulating to me. It makes me feel like I've ruined my life. But, I still have hope, I mean I can change, I hear. I've heard psychologists talk about neuroplasticity, that itself gives me hope, miracles aside."

Neuroplasticity

Neurologists define neuroplasticity as the ability of the brain to build and rebuild connections. Due to this, after stopping pornography use, the brain is able to reboot itself, albeit slowly, to return to its normal way of functioning. This neuroplasticity effect is something that neurologists have found in the brains of people who stop using pornography, where their brain begins to reboot to its originally designed way of functioning. But it isn't easy. Professor Wilson reports that several studies examining brain scans of pornography users (not addicts, but users) found that with increasing porn use comes a weaker brain, a reduced sense of reward from everyday activities, and weaker willpower. Therein lies one of the insidious elements of porn, it hooks a man and with more use, weakens his ability to leave it behind. After prolonged pornography use, the reward system in the brain simply wears out.

Professor Wilson also reports a wide variety of harms from porn including "depression, anxiety, stress, and social malfunctioning, as well as less sexual and relationship satisfaction and altered sexual tastes, poorer quality of life and health, and real-life intimacy problems." (p. 20). Of course, none of this is desirable.

An addicted condition is not without hope, however. Professor Wilson notes that recovery from an addiction to pornography can occur thanks to the neuroplasticity of the brain. The process obviously necessitates abstinence from viewing pornography. This can take between two and six months, in a process called rebooting. So what is the process like within the brain when a person views pornography? Dr. William Struthers, noted in a recent article that,

> "The human body consumes and digests food. In a similar way, we can think about the brain as a consumer of stimuli and information. When we eat, food is broken down by the digestive system and used to supply the body with the energy it needs to survive and thrive. Once it has been fully digested, whatever that is unusable (waste) is excreted. This helps to ensure the healthy functioning of the organism. If we take this analogy and extend it to the brain, the brain's job is to consume and digest information. This information is taken in through the eyes and other senses and digested and stored with meaning and memories. Anything that might have strong emotional content or is highlighted as being important information is stored and used later. The brain doesn't always get to decide what it wants to keep and what it doesn't. Sexual images are inherently powerful and have emotional content. As such, pornography forces itself on the brain. Whether one consents or not, pornography becomes a part of the fabric of the mind." He continued, "The plasticity of the beautiful, complex brain can be a blessing or a curse. While the brain is malleable, it typically follows a set of rules in performing its functions. These rules govern how connections are made, how images are processed, how behaviors are executed, and how emotions are triggered. It is here in some of these circuits that pornography seems to be exploiting one of the brain's Achilles' heels: the naked human

form. There are few things in the world that can grab someone's attention like the naked human body, and fewer still than naked bodies engaged in an intimate sexual act. One need look no further than prime time television, DVD sales, and the most frequently viewed websites to see that a great amount of time, energy, and resources take advantage of this fact of life. Sexuality and nakedness are used to entice us to watch, to buy, to follow, and to arouse us to any number of other actions. Our sexual nature provides a powerful impulse that tends to drive us. While it is true that not everyone who looks at sexually explicit images develops addictive or compulsive patterns of consumption and acting out, it is important to note that these images of nakedness and sexuality tap into a reflexive arousal response in many men, which can lead to devastating outcomes."[48]

Porn Can Be Addictive

So all this leads to a question many men have. How do I know if I am addicted to pornography? Professor Wilson ascribes to the "3 C Theory" – craving, (loss of) control, and (negative) consequences. With *craving*, someone becomes focused on getting, using, or getting over the use of a substance or experience. As behavior becomes less under the *control* of the individual, they use the substance for longer periods of time and more frequently, largely due to their increased level of tolerance. They then experience the *consequences* that come with addiction – physical, interpersonal, work, financial, and psychological problems.[49]

Greg commented on his struggle with pornography addiction.

"It's an addiction and it is the worst thing that has ever happened to me and definitely the hardest thing I've faced in my whole life; I have kind of faced it my whole life (long pause). But I have hope, because I know I'm not meant to be that way and I think it is a spiritual issue. I'm making a choice to allow myself to be exploited spiritually and economically by forces in Miami and in southern California and in New York, and I think there is something similar spiritual going on, that is what I am up against. On the other hand I have friends who love me and will accept me in spite of that with whom I can talk openly about things. And I think God wants me to be free from pornography and masturbation and I've seen him allow me to be. Whatever happens mysteriously with free will, his grace, and providence, freedom is possible and it happened this year; it was an encouraging time in the spring and it was very victorious and I've seen it and I know it can happen."

Digging deeper into this brain phenomenon, a group of neurologists studied more brain scans of people who use pornography. They used an experimental design in order to demonstrate cause and effect. They found that people who use more pornography become less able to wait for gratification than people who use less pornography. Because Internet pornography supplies a never-ending supply of potential visual rewards and given that sexual rewards are so strongly reinforcing (due to dopamine), the brain becomes retrained to demand more rewards earlier, rather than waiting for better rewards later.[50]

Over time, there has been a great deal of controversy about whether pornography use can really be called an addiction.[51] The answer from neurologists who study this phenomenon is clear: yes, pornography has the power to be addictive for some people.[52][53] Additional studies have found that some of the people most likely to become addicted are those who try to use sexual activity to get themselves out of undesirable emotional states or to reduce stress.[54]

The group of researchers who are best known for trying hardest to argue that pornography addiction doesn't exist is a small group of psychologists and a psychiatrist. Although they are not neurologists, they attempted a study looking at brain images, and try to argue that the brain scans they studied show that pornography is not addictive. However, when reviewed by neurologists, it turns out those brain images showed the opposite: pornography is addictive![55]

A group led by Dr. Vaughn Steele makes the "pornography is not addictive" argument. Their perspective is that people who are diagnosed with an addiction to pornography actually just have higher sexual desire than most people.[56] Their study looked at EEG images (brain scans) of about 50 people who believed they were viewing pornography too frequently. Based on the hypothesis that the participants were really experiencing high sexual desire, the researchers looked to demonstrate this conclusion by examining the brain waves their participants had while looking at pornography versus mundane images. When people's brains responded in a way that made the EEGs looked odd, Dr. Steele thought that they must not be addicted to pornography but rather just had high sexual desire. When neurologists looked at the findings, they saw clearly that the brainwaves these people were experiencing were completely consistent with addiction.[57] So when people who specialize in the brain's function look at the brainwaves of the participants who were watching pornography, these neurologists confidently tell us that the participants were, in fact, addicted.

I had the chance to interview one of the authors of many studies about the addictive nature of pornography, Dr. Donald Hilton. He told me that his research on addiction has shown that it is "a continued engagement in a self-destructive behavior despite adverse consequence." He added that we now know much more about how the brain operates with someone suffering from addiction. He said:

> "I believe addiction is informed by increased understanding of how the synaptic transmission occurs and how it is modified with learning and particularly with reward learning. So now, addiction is more about neuronal receptor change as it is about behavior alone … … so in other words we need to consider not only what the behavior is doing but what is the brain doing. And now of course we know that whether it is a behavioral addiction or a substance addiction, very similar changes are occurring in the reward centers. It has been striking how that is then confirmed with numerous behavioral addictions and more pertinent to what we are talking about now, specifically with regard to pornography addiction within the last year."

Further research looking at brain responses during an MRI, another method of imaging the brain, has found strong evidence of addiction by showing different responses to wanting and liking an image. Addicts tend to want it more than others, but like it just the same. The brains of addicts "fired up" in places where the same type of pattern occur with people addicted to drugs. Those who were not addicted to porn had different, normal responses.[58]

One research participant I interviewed for this book, Paul, had no trouble labeling his pornography use as an addiction. Paul is a very mature 19-year-old male with an athletic build and attractive features. He comes across as bright, sincere, and profoundly humble. When I met him, he was eager to tell his story of overcoming, yet still living with, a porn addiction. It has been two years since he has last seen pornography.

> "I can distinctly remember coming out of the bathroom (after having self-stimulated to pornography like most days) and my Dad was napping and I was at my bottom, lowest, lowest point, I just went up to him, woke him up, and just said 'I'm addicted to porn and I need help,' and it just went from there. I recognized I was addicted around 16. I'm still addicted now. That is my big struggle, for me it is lust, it is like a constant battle because it is so hard to guard your eyes because society itself is so just full of sexual immorality and it is almost just the ok thing to do in society. I still struggle with it, but not as much as before. I have no way to see it at my computer or my phone."

Paul's Dad was a good source of support for him to turn to in his struggle. His father knew that struggle well from his own life. In fact, it caused him to lose his job working at a school. He knew the consequences this addiction can have in a painful way.

Another study of the brain that has just been released, according to Dr. Donald Hilton, is research showing that the more people watch pornography each week, the more their brains shrink. Related research has also shown that viewing pornography slows down the working memory of people who view it, in other words, your short-term memory.[59] So yes, if you thought that porn makes you less intelligent, there is now evidence from neurologists to support that conclusion. Consistent with this line of research is another study that found decreased grey matter in the brain in the areas responsible for motivation and decision-making. This study, not on porn addicts but simply on male users of pornography, was among the first to find brain changes in those not addicted but who are using pornography.[60]

A Closing Thought

Essentially, pornography does a better job exciting the user than it does satisfying him. It affects the two pleasure centers in the brain differently. The excitement center fires up when one has an appetite for sex, food, or something similarly rewarding. The excitement center is primarily related to dopamine. The other system, the satisfaction center, deals with actually having sex, a meal, or something else similarly rewarding. Its most relevant brain chemical, also called a neurotransmitter, is natural endorphins, which are like the body's opiates. Internet pornography provides an infinite number of sexual objects, thus stimulating the appetite system. The result of continued, addictive use of porn is that the plasticity in the brain alters their brain's road maps, and they can't help continuing to seek more and more extreme pornography, for more and more dopamine, even though they become less and less satisfying. This is the vicious cycle that devastates people who are addicted to pornography.[61]

Chapter 4

The Link Between Pornography and Sexual Violence

When a person views pornography, does it cause him to rape? The answer to that question is complex. Of course, not every person who looks at porn commits rape; that is obvious. However, are pornography and rape strongly associated? The bulk of social science research suggests that they are. This is a question we will take up in this chapter. Before you read further, I advise you to use discretion and exercise self-care about whether you wish to continue reading. There are descriptions of sexual assault in this chapter, contextualized so that I can explain what is in pornography. Use caution if you decide to read this chapter further, especially if your life has been directly impacted by sexual violence.

We may never have a direct, definitive answer to the question of whether pornography viewing causes rape. Indeed, we can't say that pornography is a *direct* cause of rape for every person, because many more men have watched pornography than have committed rape.[62] [63] However, there are over a hundred (100+) studies showing that pornography use is both correlated with and is the cause of a wide range of violent behaviors; about 50 studies show a strong connection between pornography and sexual violence.[64] [65] Researchers have also found that pornography use increases the likelihood that a man will commit sexual violence against a woman, particularly if the man has other risk factors for committing sexual violence like being impulsive, and if his use of pornography is frequent.[66] Why might all of this be so?

A Recipe for Sexual Violence

Dr. Neil Malamuth, a social psychologist at UCLA, conducted a classic study connecting pornography and sexual violence. Dr. Malamuth found for men who are at high risk for committing sexual violence, violent pornography activates something evil within them. Two characteristics of men that are strongly associated with committing sexual assault are hostile masculinity and a preference for impersonal sex. For men with hostile masculinity and a preference for impersonal sex, pornography exposure can trigger their aggressive response. Unlike other men, these high-risk men see sexually violent media and are then motivated to be sexually aggressive, and sometimes, commit rape.[67]

The script of mainstream pornography is one of men being violent toward women. How do we know? The leading researcher about the content of today's pornography is Dr. Ana Bridges, a professor of psychology at the University of Arkansas. Dr. Bridges is an author of one of the most prominent studies of pornography ever undertaken. She and her research team purchased the most popular pornography videos in the mid 2000's. They methodically watched each one, coding the behavior that occurred in every scene of every movie. They found critically important implications for our understanding of pornography.

Each pornography movie had several scenes – perhaps a dozen or more. In 88% of the scenes – not just the movies, but the scenes in these movies – there was verbal or physical aggression, usually toward a woman. What is even more interesting is the result of this violence, as scripted by the pornography industry. When there is aggressive talk or behavior toward someone in porn, 95% of the time, the target expresses pleasure or has no response at all. This teaches viewers that people enjoy being hit. It also teaches viewers that if they are hit during a sexual encounter, they should like it, or at least not object. Think about how an 11-year-old boy, or girl, would interpret what they see. If a woman is hit, she likes it. Pornography teaches boys to hit girls, and shows girls that they should like it. That is why pornography is a recipe for sexual violence.

What Kind of Violence?

How can so much violence be depicted in mainstream pornography? Right now the pornography industry is having a difficult time keeping up with the demand from heterosexual men for pornography that degrades and brutalizes women.[68] Recently, I interviewed Dr. Ana Bridges and asked her about the violence she found in pornography. She pointed out that,

> "in pornography its awesome, everything is great, everything is orgasmically pleasing ... ... There is a lot of from my perspective that hides the violence. So all of this agreement all of this masks the true aggression that is happening in porn. Most humans have some degree of empathy and would not like becoming aroused to someone's screams of pain or protest. I think most people are decent people, and I think pornography is a way to sell aggression to people who are fundamentally decent. So how do you do that? You have to make it look like it is not aggression. And you do that through victim response."

Much like in the research done by Dr. Bridges, another psychologist, Dr. Mary Ann Layden, found evidence of violence toward women by male pornography users. Dr. Layden notes that if men are hostile toward women, are sexually promiscuous, and use pornography frequently, they are much more likely to be both physically and sexually aggressive with women. Layden summarizes her findings by noting that porn teaches, gives permission, and triggers several behaviors and attitudes that are harmful to the user and to others. This damage is seen regardless of sex or age. She notes "pornography is a widely influential and very toxic teacher."[69]

Does Pornography Make Rape More Inviting?

Dr. Robert Jensen, a professor of Journalism at the University of Texas who we met earlier in this book, told me in an interview,

> "The question used to be 'does pornography cause rape?' I've always thought that was the wrong question. It's sort of like asking what causes crime. Well you talk to a criminologist you aren't going to get a simple answer ... the question I ask is 'does pornography make rape inviting?' If you ask does pornography cause rape, either as a necessary or sufficient condition, the answer is no. If you ask whether pornography makes rape more inviting, it opens up a more interesting conversation about how men are socialized to understand sex in their relationship to women. Then you can look at patterns in the way that the pornography industry produces images and patterns in the ways men use pornography both from men's own reports of pornography or from women's reports of how pornography is used (in their relationships)."

Several of the men I interviewed as research participants for this book described the pornography they watched in way that was consistent with Dr. Jensen's view of rape as being inviting in pornography. They talked about watching a scene in a porn movie where a male would try to have sex with a woman, she would resist, he would push against her objections, and she would end up enjoying the sexual activity. Some of my participants wondered if some of the video clips they had seen might even have been real cases of sexual assault that were filmed against the woman's will. Their descriptions of what they saw, particularly in the "home made" porn often uploaded by amateurs surely seem like recorded sexual violence.

For example, Henry is an 18-year-old college student in his first semester. He is average height, Hispanic, overweight, and comes across as socially awkward. He had a difficult time looking me in the eye during our interview. He is not particularly religious. He hails from a suburb of a major city on the West Coast of the U.S. When I asked him if he had seen pornography that depicted rape, he said, "I believe I have. Of course at first it was just shock and awe, like why is he doing this. She is supposed to seem helpless and probably you are supposed to forget that she didn't want this." When I asked him why such pornography existed, he responded, "There is someone out there that enjoys watching someone brutally raped, but a majority just want to see sex. The majority might be turned off by just watching someone being brutally raped."

Henry saw this kind of pornography while watching alone. Others watched this kind of pornography in groups. Research by Dr. Walter DeKeseredy has shown that pornography teaches men to think of women as objects, not as people. A similar study found that the more men view pornography, the more they think that women are lesser creatures who they can dominate.[70]

Watching pornography that demeans women is often a group event.[71] [72] One man who learned these lessons in a group setting is "Jack." Jack is a Caucasian male about to turn 40 who teaches classes at his local college. He served as president of his fraternity, a group with a large national membership, years ago as a college student. He is unmarried, lives alone, and considers himself spiritual but not religious. He comes across as boisterous and overbearing. He described one situation in his college days when a porn movie was on in the room in which he and his friends were playing cards.

> "The guy (actor) comes in and, you know, usually the guy breaks into the house or he is let in for another reason and he starts being the aggressor and she is like 'no, no, no!' And all of the sudden she starts being like 'yes, yes, yes!' All that type of stuff. There are two kinds of those situations. There is one kind where you can tell that they are acting; it is cheesy. Then there is one that I've seen where, you knew it was acting, but it almost looked like they were trying to recreate a rape scene, and that one I couldn't finish watching. It looked like it was being recorded from a video camera, it looked like it was really happening, at no point did she ever say yes, it was more like 'no, no, no!' They had her crying through it, so it was like one of those, the guy was forcing her to the ground, I don't know if he actually was hurting her but they made it look like he was hurting her."

Jack talked about leaving the room when it was clear that the movie showed a rape. One thing I found interesting about my conversation with him is that he didn't use his leadership position (as president) to say anything to the other guys in the room about the fact that a rape was being shown on their TV. It is also relevant that after Jack left the room, everyone else stayed and casually played cards throughout the film, rape scene and all.

Another research participant, Sarah, is a 19-year-old female, Caucasian sophomore in college. She is relatively unconnected to her campus and is not particularly involved in a faith community. Sarah noted that when she looks for pornography clips on the Internet, she sometimes comes across rape scenes. She noted,

> "If I see stuff like that usually I'll stop watching it because it will make me feel uncomfortable. This could be a video that she didn't consent to or something like that. I feel bad for the girl because she might not even know that this video took place of her. Or she just might not have realized everything that was going to happen in it so I just like feel bad because she doesn't have control in the situation." When I asked her what she thought the impact of these kinds of scenes might be on men, she noted, "I think guys just think they can act just like these [movies] are. They think they can act like that, that it [sex] will just happen. It's more just like abuse and rape if both parties aren't consenting to the act."

It is noteworthy that Sarah wasn't sure that the girl experiencing rape knew that the video was being taken. This suggests that Sarah may indeed have been watching a rape in real life, rather than one that was acted out.

A Real Example

A recent longitudinal study just found that when men use more pornography during college, they are also more likely to commit sexually violent acts.[73] That relates to the experience of one of my interviewees,

John, a Caucasian male in his 20s. His dark hair and olive complexion sit atop a fit but not overly athletic physique. He was several years past his undergraduate experience at the time we spoke; he attended a mid-sized college in the Midwest. He is loosely involved in the Catholic Church. He does not embrace a Biblical worldview. Consistent with a secular worldview, I asked him if he had ever been in a situation where he thought he might not have the consent to engage in sexual activity with someone he was with intimately. He recounted this story,

> "We went back to her apartment and we were making out and the next thing you know we were going to have sex … I didn't know if she wanted to have sex but we just kept making out and next thing you know [there was sex]. She had a lot to drink. She was fine to walk, but she would have blown over the legal [driving] limit."

I asked John if pornography affected him in the decisions he made that evening. He responded,

> "Yes, because I think when you view pornography you see that men are supposed to be the aggressor and make that first move, I've never been like that until I saw porn. I would have been really shy in trying to make that first move but watching porn has given me the courage and I have become brave to make that first move so I would say yeah, definitely watching porn has made me, especially in that instance, be the aggressor and be the first person to make that first move. Because it goes back to when you feel like you are a man. Yeah, like if you define what a man is, that is the definition of what a man is right there, when you are making that first move and being a guy, being a man, having sex."

When I asked him if he thought what he did that night was legal, he said "no." John's experience is a prototype of what happens when men watch pornography and decide to act on what they have learned.

What might drive a man to look at pornography and then behave in that way? Philosopher Dr. Rebecca Whisnant notes that pornography

> "presents men as these utterly amoral robotic penetrators of essentially everything that moves, and even a few things that don't move. I think it does that partly because the male consumer has to be able to essentially imagine himself as the one who is doing the penetrating. But also there is a reason why these men have to be presented as completely amoral and devoid of empathy, because if they weren't they wouldn't be able to do what they are doing, and when the male consumer does identify with them he needs to be able to identify with someone who is unable or unwilling to see women as human beings entitled to care, or consideration, or respect."

Different People, Different Effects

Many studies have demonstrated that the use of pornography is associated with men's violence against women. One thing that is important about this line of research is that pornography does not affect all viewers in the same way. Recent research by an international team of scholars found that only men with a high risk-level for committing violence had their attitudes toward that violence changed by increasing use of pornography. Of course men who have low risk for committing violence still experience effects from their viewing of pornography as discussed throughout this book. However, this particular study found that men who are already at a high risk for committing sexual assault and who also frequently use pornography have the strongest attitudes supporting violence against women. Interestingly, men who have a high risk of committing sexual assault but watch pornography seldom or never had attitudes toward sexual violence that were less supportive of sexual violence than similar men who frequently viewed porn. So pornography use seems to have its own impact in this context.[74]

A popular theory explaining why some men commit sexual assault found that men who are hostile toward women and prefer impersonal, promiscuous sex are more likely to commit rape. A recent study examined how men who were high in these two characteristics related to their pornography use. The researchers found that men who believed more strongly in impersonal, promiscuous sex and were hostile toward women were more likely to sexually assault a woman if they frequently used pornography. In addition, men with these two characteristics were more likely to prefer violent pornography.[75] In a related study, men who prefer violent pornography were found to be less intelligent, have more internal hostility, prefer sex to be impersonal rather than relational, and have both antisocial and aggressive inclinations.[76] In short, frequent pornography use by itself is not a singular, direct cause for sexual assault. However, if a man has other risk factors for committing sexual violence, for example hostile masculinity or a preference for impersonal sex, adding frequent pornography use makes it significantly more likely that he will commit sexual violence.[77]

Other research looking at what promotes attitudes in support of violence against women found that the more antagonistic, unfriendly, and self-interested men are, the more likely that their watching pornography will lead to stronger attitudes supporting violence against women. Men who were not antagonistic, were friendly and not so self-interested were not as affected by the violent messages in pornography.[78]

In a study of how pornography affects some men more than others in Germany, a team of researchers found that German men who have committed violence in the course of their sexual relations and who viewed pornography more frequently than other violent men were more likely to do a wide variety of demeaning acts toward women. Some of these acts lead women to vomit. So in other words, violent men who watch a lot of pornography are violent in more ways, and more frequently, than other men who have used violence in their sexual encounters. An interesting contribution this study made to our understanding of violence and pornography is that violent men were also more likely to drink alcohol before or during sexual encounters.[79]

The disturbing phenomenon of sexual acts that lead women to vomit is becoming increasingly common. When I interviewed Greg, he shared,

> "Honestly, the biggest porn companies and the websites and the videos you see, the most popular models, it (women vomiting from sex acts) is kind of standard issue now. You go to the website and the first page, (is going to have that). It snuck into mainstream pornography; it is sadomasochistic. There is still this other genre that is sadomasochism … where they try to make girls vomit and stuff. Even that stuff in mainstream videos is what scared me … … It is just inherently violent; it is chauvinistic. It is terrifying that I would enjoy that. It was terrifying because I knew it was wrong, I knew it was a human being on the screen, just the pleasure though that came along with that. I don't know why I liked it. I think that it is because sexuality is so primal; I think violence is also primal. And I think there is some relationship inherently

deep down between the two." He continued, "I think it (violence) becomes sexually exciting, I think I could if I get rid of my conscience, and just gave myself over to that, I could follow that rabbit hole and love every minute of it. I just think, I don't understand sadomasochism really or why violence is bound up in this, I just think it is part of man's primitive nature, the deepest part of the id, sin, fallenness, whatever you want to call it. I call it sin. It just comes out there. It is in me. It is in anybody who wants to give themselves over to it. I just think they are tied together."

Wife Abuse

Another area in which pornography use seems to impact violence against women is within the context of domestic violence. Several studies have looked at whether men's use of pornography has an impact on their physical abuse of wives or live-in partners. The researcher who has done the most work in this area is Dr. Walter DeKeseredy. Among divorced couples he studied, 30% said that their husband's pornography viewing was integral to the sexual abuse they experienced in their marriage.[80] When I interviewed Dr. DeKeseredy, he explained it this way, "pornography kept coming up in the interviews [with women]. This is one of the most powerful determinants." A researcher who worked with him, Dr. Mandy Hall-Sanchez, continued this line of research with women in rural settings in Ohio. According to Dr. DeKeseredy, she found that "the women she interviewed went on and on and on about pornography and talked about how much it was part and parcel of their ex-partners lives and how much their partners were connected with other men who used it."

Just a Correlation?

Some people dismiss studies connecting pornography and sexual violence as merely correlational. Setting aside for the moment that many of these studies use research methods that can show cause and effect relationships, correlational studies remain critically important. In my interview with the Director of the Psychopathology program at the University of Pennsylvania, Dr. Mary Anne Layden, she noted that critics of the pornography research say things like "well these are correlational studies and correlation does not imply causality." Her response to this criticism is telling.

> "Oh dear, I guess you don't actually believe that cigarette smoking causes cancer since all that research is correlational and we don't have any experimental studies on cigarette smoking! So I guess you tell your children go ahead and smoke cigarettes because we don't have anything that says cigarettes causes cancer or all the other things they cause. So if you do think cigarettes cause cancer, are you aware that there are only correlational studies, that it would be unethical to do experimental studies with cigarettes. Like we got 2 groups of 3rd graders and we are going to make one group smoke and one not and see how long it takes to kill them? We won't be doing that! Or you don't actually believe that drunk driving causes accidents, because all of that research is correlational as well."

Indeed, just because two things occur together it doesn't mean one caused the other. However, when you have over 100 studies that show that pornography use is associated with a variety of violent behaviors, how many more studies does the reasonable person need to conclude that something is going on here? In fact, there have been laboratory studies done using methods that can show causality. And they show substantial harm to the user. Fortunately for our knowledge base, we don't need to rely simply on correlational studies to show how pornography and sexual violence intersect.

Dr. Paul Wright and his research team released a study just as this book was going into print. They analyzed recent data on pornography use and sexual violence from 22 studies and 7 different nations. They found that in correlational, cross-sectional, and longitudinal studies, pornography use and acts of sexual aggression were directly connected. This connection held true for both men and women, and for verbal and physical aggression. Violent pornography was even more strongly linked to sexual violence.[81] Moreover, after reviewing over 500 studies to determine whether consumption of pornography causes gender based violence, Dr. Max Waltman of Stockholm University concluded that the weight of the evidence shows the direction of the connection clearly.[82] He noted that the available research shows that pornography causes gender based violence through most every methodology imaginable, using experimental and nonexperimental studies, quantitative and qualitative studies, and samples of specific groups and samples of the general population. Dr. Waltman describes the effects as not only statistically significant but robust.

A Concluding Thought

In closing this chapter, I note that Victor Malerek, author of *The Johns: Sex for sale and the men who buy it*[83], pointed out that pornography and sex buying (by "Johns") are commonly associated. He notes "Porn is often what turns the men on, revs up their sex drive, and sends them out into the night." (p 193). Quoting one porn producer and actor who commented on the connection between pornography and violence, Malerek was told how the pornographer demeans women in vile and almost unspeakable ways. The same pornographer makes films to help pedophiles know how to rape a child. Is this what you have in mind when you think of today's pornography?

After reading this chapter, I hope you have gained a more complete understanding of the violence that is endemic to pornography. I also hope that it has given you a newfound sense of urgency to keep yourself, and those you love, away from what the pornography industry is trying to sell us. And bear in mind, the information from the pornography producer above is now at least 10 years old, and the porn industry has kept upping the ante on the kind of violence in its movies ever since.

Chapter 5

How The Porn Use of Others May Affect You

If you are a person who rarely if ever views pornography, you may find it surprising to hear how frequently people in the general population look at it. In addition to many of the statistics we discussed in chapter 1, much more is now known about the vast reach of pornographic images. One of the ways that some (but not all) people search for pornography is through gateway websites, which categorize various types of pornography that people wish to access. There are many such sites. By looking at the usage data from just one of these many gateway websites, we can begin to understand the vast reach of pornography.

In 2014, just one of the many available gateway websites reported that people viewed 79 billion videos through their site that year. To put that into perspective, that is 11 videos for every person on earth. Thus, those actually accessing the site are viewing massive quantities of porn, very frequently. In 2014, over 18 billion visits were made to their site; 5,800 per second. The United States had more users on the site than any other nation. In one year, there were 123 page views for every person in the United States. Again, because not all people are using porn, and not all people who do access that one site, those who are visiting look at a staggering number of images. Usage of the site is increasing dramatically. The 79 billion videos viewed in 2014 are up from 63 billion the year before. Reflecting the porn industry's efforts to get people sexually interested in younger and younger performers, the number one search term in 2014 was "teen." "Teen" was followed by 'lesbian' and several other terms referring to pornography where young males engage in sex with women old enough to be their mother. The search term 'lesbian' was used more often by female visitors to the site than it was used by the males. Women also search frequently for 'gay male,' while men are more likely to search for 'anal.' For the first time, smart phones surpassed computers as the most common device to access pornography, particularly in the United States.[84]

There are many ways research shows that the pornography use of others may affect you, whether or not you view pornography. For example, clinical psychology professor Dr. Ana Bridges has conducted several studies on the impact of pornography, including her doctoral dissertation. Through her many studies she has uncovered numerous effects of pornography – all of them harmful. With many of these harms, they don't just affect the individual, but others around them as well. For example, she found that porn use increases the viewer's feelings of contempt for women, decreases empathy for people who have survived sexual violence, lessens the user's ability to show emotion in situations where one usually would, increases dominance behaviors, increases sexually aggressive behaviors, and can be addictive. Furthermore, she found that women are hesitant to enter into relationships with men who frequently consume pornography.[85]

The harms that Dr. Bridges found are cause for concern for anyone who might use, or be around those who use, pornography. There are also many other potential and actual harms of pornography.

Philosopher Dr. Rebecca Whisnant form the University of Dayton notes two harms in particular.

> "One would be the harm that is being done to performers -- particularly though perhaps not only female performers -- in the industry who are actually involved in the making of pornography. And then the other kind would be broader social harms, harms that are in some sense the result of pornography consumption. Certainly many women are harmed by the consumption of porn, usually men, in their lives -- whether it is partners or men that they interact with socially, professionally, or on the street. When men's conception of who women are, and what women are for, and what women (enjoy) is shaped by the kind of material that we are talking about – that is not good for women."

In recognition of these many harms, this chapter is divided into sections based on the relationship you may have with an individual whose pornography use could affect you. The kinds of relationships most relevant to harm that can be done to you by others include a romantic partner, your friends, and a parent. In addition, notable harms are done to people of color by the pornography industry.

Your Romantic Partner

"Ella" is an African-American woman in her late 20's who is pursuing an advanced degree. She has a young son and identifies as a nondenominational Christian. Her experience is typical of many women whose male romantic partners use pornography. She reports,

> "I have had boyfriends that look at porn. I didn't like it, sometimes they would make me watch, too,

and I tried, but I don't like it at all. One of them was actually addicted to porn; it was an overly big problem for him and that was a really big stress on our relationship. I was uncomfortable with it as a whole; you are looking at another girl, that whole thing. From a spirituality perspective I don't agree with it at all and I saw that it had a hold over him and if we were going to go further in our relationship, I didn't want that to be a part of my life, my son wasn't here yet, but if we were still together, I wouldn't want him exposed to it [from my boyfriend] and if we were to get married I didn't want to be married to someone who was addicted to porn. So yeah, it just caused stress."

Ella's experience is consistent with research done by Dr. Bridges. Dr. Bridges has found in her research that when someone uses pornography, they feel insecure about their relationship and their partner. Not surprisingly, she also found that the more people use pornography, the less they are satisfied with their partners. This impact is likely due to looking at pictures of so many other people that unfavorable comparisons are made to their partner's physique. A sizeable number of women in Dr. Bridges' study reported insecurity about their body and themselves if they viewed pornography.[86]

Dr. Bridges is part of a research team that has recently conducted several studies about how pornography use affects romantic relationships. The others who worked with her were Dr. Chyng Sun from New York University, Dr. Matt Ezzel from James Madison University, and Dr. Jennifer Johnson from Virginia Commonwealth University. At the time this book went to press, not all of their research had been published, so what I report here can be considered preliminary results and a preview of research that will be released soon after this book is published.

They found different impacts for men and women, regarding their relationships. They found that the more pornography men viewed, the less satisfied they were with their partner. This effect seems likely due to comparing the physical attractiveness of their partner with women in pornography. In addition, men who used porn very frequently had less satisfaction with their partner in general and in the sexual aspect of their relationship. If their partner viewed pornography, men's satisfaction with their partner was higher.

When men and women were asked why they used pornography, Dr. Bridges reports that for men, the top reason was to facilitate masturbation. For women, their top reason was because they incorporate it into sex with their partner. Dr. Bridges notes

> "it is not a surprise that the more their female partners are using porn, because they are primarily using it in a context of sexual activity with a partner, the more men say, 'Yup, everything is great, love my partner, love my sex life, everything is great.' In women, it's a slightly different story. Women's pornography use was not at all related to their happiness in their relationship or happiness in their sex life. But the more their male partners used porn, the less satisfied they were. When you see how porn is being used, it is different in men and women, it makes more sense."

Dr. Bridges' confirmed the results of several earlier studies. In one study published in the *Journal of Social and Clinical Psychology*, a research team found that when people use pornography more frequently, their satisfaction in their couple relationship declined.[87] Pornography users were also less committed to their romantic partner and were more likely to have sex with another person while still in the relationship with their partner. Similarly, another research team found that the more men use pornography, the less they, and their wives or partners, are satisfied with their sexual relationship.[88]

This use of pornography by a man affecting his partner is reflected in the experience of Kaitlin. Kaitlin is a 22-year-old junior in college who identifies as a nondenominational Christian, though like many her age, her sexual behavior is not consistent with church teaching. She reported her discomfort with her boyfriend's use of pornography.

> "My boyfriend, he would always delete his history on his phone. I never asked him but if I would like sit down and think about it, it would make me feel uncomfortable feeling like I'm supposed to be with my boyfriend, and we are sexually active, and then he goes and he watches other people who have sex or whatever he watches. That makes me feel uncomfortable. It was definitely not something that I would want my boyfriend to do."

I asked others about how pornography affects relationships, including Dr. Robert Jensen, a professor of journalism at the University of Texas. He noted that in his conversations with both therapists and divorce lawyers, he has seen a pattern, in that they note an

> "increase in the number of clients they see in which some significant part of the dissolution of the marriage was the man's habitual use of pornography" and "sexual aggression that is increasing, the pattern is pretty clear. When you take that kind of anecdotal evidence, one or two stories don't make a pattern, but when a pattern emerges, it is evidence. When you combine that with what we do know from the laboratory evidence, what seems to be clear, for men who have a predisposition to sexual aggression,

use of pornography, especially the more aggressive pornography, likely increases sexual violence. That is the minimal conclusion."

A researcher who has perhaps published the greatest number of studies about pornography during the last few years is Dr. Paul Wright, an Assistant Professor in the Media School at Indiana University. In a study he conducted with Dr. Ashley Randall, they looked at men's potential health outcomes from their pornography use. In particular, Dr. Wright was concerned with the spread of sexually transmitted infections (STIs), given that many behaviors demonstrated in pornography are high-risk behaviors. Dr. Wright found, using a nationwide sample of adults, that the more men viewed Internet pornography, the more they had sex with multiple partners and had sex with a prostituted woman. Furthermore, married men who used Internet pornography were more likely to cheat on their spouses.[89]

Later, in a study with over 20,000 men Dr. Wright conducted with Dr. Robert Tokunaga, they found that the more men view media where women are treated as objects rather than as people, the more they thought that women really were merely *things* that existed to sexually please men. In addition, the more men thought of women as objects, the more they also supported violence against women.[90] Sociologists Walter DeKeseredy and Martin Schwartz note that pornography teaches men to think of women as objects, not as people. These lessons to think of women as lesser than a person often occur in the context of group pornography viewing. In their study of rural women who survived sexual assault during their separation or divorce from their husbands, DeKeseredy & Schwartz noted that the former husbands of these women frequently viewed pornography with their male friends. Nearly a third of these women stated that pornography was directly involved in the sexual abuse their husbands

John D. Foubert, Ph.D.

committed against them.[91] In my interview with philosopher Dr. Rebecca Whisnant, she observed,

> "Pornography is incredibly objectifying of both men and women. For women it is not hard to see. The kind of things that women are called in pornography is one easy way. If you call someone a (sexually explicit name) it's not only reducing someone to their sexual parts; it is even worse than that because it is reducing someone to a profoundly negative and denigrating conception of their sexual parts and their sexual functions."

Your Friends

For the last several years, I have engaged in several studies examining the effects pornography has on whether or not people choose to help someone during an emergency situation. In particular, I've been interested to find out whether consuming violent pornography affects whether people will intervene to help prevent a rape from happening when it looks like it could occur.

My first two studies, done with a research team that included Dr. Matt Brosi, Dr. Sean Bannon, and Gabriel Yandell, looked at how pornography use impacted whether college fraternity and sorority members would intervene to help someone when it looked like a person might be sexually assaulted. In two studies, we found that if people were viewers of violent pornography, they were less likely to intervene to help a friend.[92][93] Relatively high levels of pornography use were shown for each group, with 83% of fraternity men and 46% of sorority women viewing pornography in the last year. In our studies, we looked specifically at violent pornography, pornography that was either sadomasochistic or showed rape happening. We found that 21% of sorority women had viewed sadomasochistic pornography. If women were among those who viewed sadomasochistic porn, they were more likely to believe that they were incapable of intervening and were also less willing to intervene, regardless of how capable they felt. Our study of fraternity men found that the 27% of men who viewed sadomasochistic pornography in the last year reported less likelihood of knowing what to do to help prevent a sexual assault if they saw one about to happen. The 19% of fraternity men who viewed rape pornography in the previous year were less willing to intervene to help someone who might be sexually assaulted, regardless of how capable they believed they were to do so.

Together, these studies demonstrated that when college students who are part of Greek organizations take part in viewing pornography, they are less likely to help a friend who may be sexually assaulted. We believe that these results emerged because of the influence that pornography has. If someone views violence mixed with sexual images, they become less likely to see the violence in those images as problematic. If they are less likely to see violence as a problem, they are then less likely to intervene to stop it from happening. We also believe that these studies demonstrate that the impact of pornography use isn't just on the viewer. Rather, it can also extend to people who are friends or acquaintances of the viewer, because their pornography-viewing friend is less likely to help them out of the toughest of situations.

As a follow-up to these studies, I collaborated with Dr. Ana Bridges. We surveyed participants from two universities, and sampled a diverse range of students, not just those in fraternities and sororities. In an article we have coming out soon in the *Journal of Interpersonal Violence,*[94] we found that both men and women who report a greater variety of motives for viewing pornography are less willing to intervene in a situation where someone may experience rape than participants with fewer motives to view pornography. Specifically, we found that people who have the following motives express lower willingness to intervene: "to make sex more interesting," "to enjoy a social event," "for sexual thrills," and "to learn about sex." The other major thing we found is that men and women were equally likely to use pornography to turn on a sexual partner. With all other motivations to use pornography, men far surpassed women. This finding confirms reports from women that they use pornography, at the request of their partners, to sexually excite their partner.

In another follow-up to my original studies on pornography, I worked with my colleage Andrew Rizzo to explore the likelihood that people would intervene to help someone who is in danger of being sexually assaulted. We found that both men and women who are motivated to be religious for their own personal gain and social standing were less likely to help someone in danger of experiencing rape. Thus, being around more self-centered friends can be risky.[95]

Another way that the pornography use of your friends can affect you is through the withdrawal from social networks common to men who use pornography. For example, Katie recalls a time when a good friend of hers from high school became addicted to pornography.

> "One of my really good friends from high school. We were seniors. We were all really close. He just started to drift away from us. And we thought that maybe it was because college was fixin' to happen and stuff like that. He kind of opened up to us and said, 'I got kind of addicted to watching it (pornography)' and he got help and stuff and he is better now. It made him different. He was like really open and had a very contagious attitude, he was fun to be around and then he got really reserved, shut himself off from things, it was kind of a big deal. Where we are from, it is a really small town so it is kind of a big deal when someone switches." When I

asked Katie to elaborate, she recalled "At the time I was just kinda worried about him. I didn't expect it to be because of pornography, at all, but at first I was 'what are you doing?' Why? And he finally sat down and talked to me and he said after (watching porn for awhile) he had to watch it, it was something he had to do. It wasn't just like a normal teenage guy. I was kind of thrown off guard. I didn't think any less of him because everybody struggles somewhere, I have a family member who does, but my friend lost 2 or 3 of our good friends over it because they thought it was wrong. They got really mad and kind of left. They said that is ridiculous and I'm not going to be your friend anymore."

I asked Katie to describe what she meant by her friend being addicted.

"He said he would go home and watch it everyday after work, he would go to work at 8 and he would watch it for like 4 hours a day. In the beginning he would watch it 30 minutes every 2 to 3 days and it just progressively added up to it. He went to a counselor, he saw a psychologist first. I know he saw a counselor every day. He needed to see someone every day. This is a faith-based counselor. He did that every day for 5 months. Now I think he is back down to (seeing the counselor) once a week because it has been four years.

When people are addicted to pornography, they will often spend an inordinate amount of time viewing it. Research has shown that when someone is addicted, they spend an average of 40 hours per week on the Internet; about as many hours as many full time jobs.[96]

A Parent

I imagine that most anyone would have a difficult time thinking about their parents viewing pornography, and how their parent might use it either themselves or in their marital relationship. One research participant for this book who came face to face with this impact was Paul (whom we met earlier). Paul notes,

> "My dad lost a job as a teacher in a high school because he was on porn, it was when I was in 4th grade and my brother was in 2nd grade. He had been a high school teacher and a swim coach for a long time and we transferred from school to school, and uh, he had to leave that school and it was very abrupt. I remember we (originally) had all these plans of moving to [the town where this school was located] and we were really banking on this and like his athletic program was going real high and we were banking on this, and then he got fired. He told us that he got fired and would lose his job but he wouldn't tell us why. Later on he told me that he was caught looking at porn, and that was the reason why he lost his job. It was pornographic videos I think. Yeah that was a big thing that popped out to me when I think of how pornography affected our family. And so he had to go full time giving swimming lessons at the local pool and it was rough, because I mean teachers' salaries are pretty bad anyways, but he went down from there to get paid by the number of lessons he did, I mean it affected us financially. I'm sure it also affected his relationship with mom and they had to work through that ... ...
> I'm sure it made him feel worthless and that he let us down and lost his job because of it, but it really

affects your emotional status and your interaction with other people because like you are carrying around guilt and all this stuff that goes along with it. It affects how you interact, like you can be very short tempered, not patient, always having like a chip on your shoulder. My Dad was like this and I attribute that to the pornography. It takes over the person itself. It is really hard to overcome like a stronghold it has on a person because it is very habitual to look at pornography. That lust that feeds it is hard to kind of get rid of so it is something that is just like nagging at you and it also really hurts your self-worth, at least from my experience it does. It has a control over you at times, control as in pornography is so accessible, there is kinda like a switch that you can be turned on by. What someone is saying or something on TV or something, because pornography is so accessible you can act on that."

If you are a person of color

In my interview with Dr. Robert Jensen from the University of Texas, he noted how the pornography industry affects people of color, and indeed all people who wish to live in a society free from racism. He stated,

> "There are porn videos that advertise themselves as racist. This is one where, if you look at network TV, Hollywood movies, other mass media, you can still find subtle racist patterns. Like Hollywood is still in love with young black male thugs and there is a disproportionate presence of stereotypes, but those are subtle. You have to argue out why this is a problem. You go into contemporary, mass

marketed, industrially produced pornography and the racism isn't hidden, subtle, or coded. It is right up front and is advertised. There is a genre of porn called interracial. And what interracial porn means, at the base, is that there are people in this movie who aren't white. If you pull a porn video off the shelf and it is not coded as interracial there is a pretty good chance it is all white people. What the porn industry has done is code that the presence of nonwhite people as interracial." He continued, "Most of the interracial porn is black men and white women. With very openly racist titles ... The genre itself produces and markets racist videos as racist videos. They'll tell you it is all just fantasy, but that is just the standard industry line. The evidence is pretty clear that much like in the dominant culture, nonwhite women in porn are paid less on average and relegated to a lower position in the industry on average. That seems to be pretty clear."

A Concluding Thought

University of Arkansas professor, Dr. Ana Bridges, conducted several studies showing different harms of pornography. When I interviewed Dr. Bridges, I found this comment she made as particularly poignant, and an appropriate way to demonstrate that the research on the harms of pornography can be trusted.

> "I will tell you that I did not come into this research area with an agenda. I am not religious, I don't have a particular dog in this particular race, I don't have a sordid history of a partner, I just don't have this personal tie. So I've always maintained the stance that I'm willing to go where the data go. That has

always been my stance. I remain firmly in that camp. I go where the data go. I don't try to just ask questions about everything that is wrong. Most of my outcome measures about satisfaction and about happiness and enjoyment, those are supposed to be like, 'Hey, if this is helping you, the data should show me this.' I am amazed at how over a decade of research, the data keep pointing [in] one direction and not just in my lab, across different countries with different researchers with different methods with different samples you have a pretty cohesive story emerging. I'm not invested in a particular outcome. I've tried to be as intellectually honest as I could be with my work, and here is what it seems to be saying and it is not just my stuff that is showing it. I think that is important. It is important to know that I am not agenda driven first and then go find the data to support it. I have questions and the data are telling me what they are telling me! I don't consider myself a priori anti-pornography. I consider myself pro-empiricism. I think that is important, it is central to me. You can look at some scholars and they have staked a claim. For me it is always an open question. Again, across samples, the story in general is *not* one that is very flattering to the porn industry or to ourselves as consumers."

Chapter 6

Who are these people? Motives of producers and actors in pornography.

Who are the people in the pornography industry? Why do producers and directors make pornography? Do people who perform in pornography generally want to and do they enjoy it? In this chapter, I will introduce you to some of the people who are part of the industry. What you have heard about the pornography industry is probably different from the reality of those who experience it. In the latter part of the chapter, you will have the opportunity to learn, at length, from someone who has been in many films, about what it feels like to appear in pornography. She now serves with Pink Cross, a ministry rescuing people from the porn industry.

Though being in a pornographic movie is thought by many to be lucrative, the average porn star works for a few months to possibly a few years and ends the experience with no money in their bank account. Women in the pornography industry tend to be survivors of child sexual abuse – three times as many women in the porn industry were sexually abused than in the general population.[97] Many women in pornography see their only worth as providing sexual gratification to men. Women in the porn industry are 50% more likely to be living in poverty and twice as likely as the general public to have grown up in poverty.[98]

A Producer's Perspective

Several scholars have studied people who are part of the pornography industry. One is Dr. Robert Jensen, Professor of Journalism at the University of Texas. As part of his research for the critically acclaimed book *Getting Off: Pornography and the End of Masculinity,*[99] Dr. Jensen attended a pornography industry convention (yes, the porn industry has conventions, not surprisingly in Las Vegas). One thing that struck him was the increase in male to female anal sex in pornographic movies. He asked a producer why the industry included these scenes in their movies. The producer noted that showing anal sex in his movies helps men who watch to fantasize about demeaning a woman through sexual submission. He went on to say that such scenes are filmed to show women *not* enjoying what they are doing.

In an interview with the *Daily Beast*, a former male pornography producer and actor gave an inside look at the realities of working inside the industry. Rob Zicari (stage name Rob Black) was known for producing such violent pornography that even those in the porn industry were taken aback. In a way, this was a sign of respect from fellow industry executives who keep looking for more ways to combine sexual activity and violence in their productions. Zicari's movies made with wife "Lizzy Borden" were so horrifically violent that the federal government indicted them for obscenity – an action almost never taken for adult pornography. Even more rare, Zicari and Borden received a sentence exceeding a year in prison.[100]

Black shared that people in the industry now look to cloak their extreme violence under the guise of "Bondage, Domination, Sadism, and Masochism," known by the trendy sounding term, "BDSM."

Many such movies make *50 Shades of Grey* look like a G rated children's film. For example, in one production, they put a woman on a dog chain, attached the chain to a wall, and kept her there for days. During that time, they shocked her with a cattle prod – a practice that even Black defines as torture.[101]

STIs

Even if women who appear in pornography are not shocked with a cattle prod, there are still several kinds of harm they experience, beyond the obvious spiritual harm. For example, scholars who study pornography industry performers note that sexually transmitted infections (STIs) like chlamydia and gonorrhea are very common among performers, at a rate 64 times higher than in the general population.[102] A sizeable number in the industry also have HIV. Scholars remind us that testing for STIs doesn't prevent transmission of infections, only strategies like condom use during films is likely to stem the tide.[103]

Requiring condom use is something that hit the pornography industry like an automatic braking system installed in a car that is about to crash. In fact, in late 2013 the *Los Angeles Times* reported that because of a new law mandating the use of condoms in the filming of pornography, production of pornography in LA County plummeted 95% in that one year. This sets the stage for the industry to relocate somewhere else in the U.S. or abroad.[104]

New Restrictions, New Formats

I asked Dr. Gail Dines, widely known as the leader of the secular anti-porn movement, how the new laws came about in California. She noted that the force behind new laws mandating condom use was The AIDS healthcare foundation. According to Dines,

"The AIDS healthcare foundation put the major nail in the coffin of the porn industry in the United States, and vowed to follow the porn industry all over the U.S. [to advocate for condom laws] if necessary. Now the industry will be more diffuse than it was. Some of it will go to Las Vegas. Most will go to Eastern European countries. It will make it virtually impossible to get a handle on the production side." She continued, "So what happened is now the industry has a diffuse production end. So production is still concentrated in LA, but is probably going to move. It is moving to Eastern Europe, because you have an unending supply of poor women and children and you don't have any health laws, you don't have [the Occupational Safety and Health Administration] (OSHA)."

In my interview with Dr. Dines, she noted that to understand the pornography industry, one has to understand the difference between the aforementioned production and distribution sides of their business. The production side makes the content; the distribution side makes it available to as many people as possible. One of the things she has been following lately is the activity on the distribution side. She noted that distribution of pornography

"has shifted dramatically since MindGeek came in and vacuumed up the distribution outlets ... [On] the distribution side, which is always connected to the production side, MindGeek, a Luxemburg organization with offices in San Diego, has come in and they are now buying up all of the free porn sites. The business goal is about bringing in a premium membership to free porn sites but really the money they make is through monetizing free porn by selling the real estate on the pages of the free porn sites."

Thus what has been free will increasingly move to being pay per view. And a single company is apparently moving to establish a monopoly on free pornography, in a seeming attempt to increase advertising rates on pornography sites – all for a profit that would make Bill Gates envious.

Commenting on recent trends in the pornography industry, Dr. Dines noted

> "Another big, big moneymaker that is about to hit is webcams, because webcams are real time and you can't pirate the stuff. The problem is that on MindGeek, a lot of it is pirated. A lot of the porn companies that are producing it are very upset with all the pirating. You can't pirate webcams because they are real time. The webcams are sucking up business on the free porn sites. If you go into a free porn site, you've got tons of ads for webcams. The webcam business is now becoming monopolized and consolidated through another website. Users have to pay for private sessions with the webcam women."

When new technology is introduced, it often results in expanded access to pornography.[105] In fact, much of the time, new technology has been developed and funded by the porn industry in order to sell their products more successfully.[106] If you have any idea what kind of technology is being used by people to access pornography today, you know that most people, especially young people, are accessing pornography on their mobile phones rather than on laptops. Like me, you probably didn't know all the reasons why this development is so lucrative to the pornography industry. According to Dr. Dines,

"The important thing about that is that it allows much more porn to be used in countries like India and Brazil. Prior to mobile phone access, free porn couldn't get a hold of those countries because they are typically people living in overcrowded situations where there is one computer per family in the living room. So the guys can't be masturbating (to porn) in the living room with the whole family. But with the mobile phone, they can find a quiet place and go download porn and masturbate to it. This was actually discussed in a [porn industry] conference in London four years ago, about how the mobile phone was going to open up previously closed markets in Brazil and India."

"Feminist" Porn?

One strategy the pornography industry is currently using to earn more profits is to put women in charge of making some of the movies and to label some pornography as "feminist porn." This oxymoron has been studied by Dr. Ana Bridges, who conducted research on whether there is a difference in the content between pornographic movies made by men versus those made by women. In my interview with her, she noted,

"We randomly selected from the best selling and best renting porn. Within that universe of movies, we then said do you see a difference between what women [directors] do and what men do. The answer is no, in the top selling movies, it is all aggressive, it is all directed at women, it is all very extreme, and the female directors are not more genteel and kind than the male directors ... That doesn't mean that if you looked at the universe of women directors in general you wouldn't see something different. But to make it to that top tier they have to outdo the men in their hyper-masculinity and their aggression. In that top renting tier, they are not only doing what the men do, they are doing it even more."

In my interview with philosophy professor Dr. Rebecca Whisnant, we also talked about the "feminist" porn phenomenon. She stated,

"There is certainly an element in the pornography industry that looks to make its products attractive to a broader audience by calling it 'feminist porn.' It is in the interest of the industry as a whole to have another niche market of material that labels itself feminist."

Though the producers of "feminist porn" sometimes try to publicly distance themselves from the mainstream pornography industry, in order to establish a separate identity, the reality, according to Dr. Whisnant, is that

"the relationship between many self-described feminist pornographers and the mainstream industry is very cozy, from what I can discern. For example, (female porn producer) Tristan Taormino prides herself on working hand in glove with the mainstream industry, and to her credit, she is very forthcoming about that relationship; it's not like she is trying to hide it. And she is forthcoming about the fact that this has involved certain kinds of compromises and things that she might not otherwise have done. The way that she got her first movie made is that she approached many mainstream pornographers to make it, to fund it, and finally she was able to get (a high profile male pornography producer) to do it and he was the executive producer. He is a very prominent mainstream gonzo (a more extreme form of pornography, void of any pretense of a plot) pornographer, and she goes to him, hat in hand, saying I want you to make this movie."

As to whether there are or can be pornographic films that meet a common definition of "feminist," Dr. Whisnant (a prominent feminist scholar) maintains that

"no pornography that I have ever seen, that I am aware of in any way, shape, or form, is consistent with my operational definition of what is feminist. To me, for some kind of sexual or erotic material to qualify as feminist, just for starters, it would have to exist outside what Andrea Dworkin defined as the nature and function of pornography, which is that it sexualizes hierarchy, objectification, submission, and violence. And so, basically, feminist sexual material would have to not sexualize any of those things." She continues, "But what is very clear in looking at the materials and the writings of these people who fancy themselves feminist pornographers or feminist porn performers is what I've described here has nothing to do with their conception of what feminist porn is. Their conception of feminist porn is completely consistent with the sexualizing of hierarchy, objectification, submission, and violence—including, though not limited to, material in which women bear the brunt of these practices."

So, what are the markers of the pornographic genre that identifies as "feminist porn?" Dr. Whisnant reports,

> "What makes the difference to them, what makes material 'feminist' in their view, is authenticity. That is, it's not scripted, it is not fake, it represents the real desires of the people who are performing, particularly the women. Another element that is supposed to make 'feminist porn' different is mixing up roles and representations, so that it is not always men shown being dominant and women in a submissive role."

The Reality of Being Filmed

So who are the actors who appear in pornography? Dr. Robert Jensen notes,

> "Young women come to the valley of southern California, although, now production is leaving California, often in the old days, a high percentage of porn production was in the San Fernando Valley of southern California. Young women come and the industry chews up and spits out women at an alarming rate. So you come, you work, the work is so brutal, it is so psychologically and physically taxing that you leave quickly and maybe you have made a few thousand dollars, who knows?"

Research on pornography performers undercuts the notion that acting in porn is lucrative. The overwhelming majority of the people who appear in the porn industry are unsuccessful in the industry for any length of time.[107] While they are in the industry, Dr. Jensen notes,

"We know that drug and alcohol abuse is unusually high in the sexual exploitation industries. So, what people make is often to feed these habits. There are women who make a living in porn. The more well-known performers who can command higher fees and are sensible enough to manage their money wisely, they are probably making a middle class living or better. But the question is, of the thousands of women who cycle through the industry every year, how many of them are making money like that every year. My guess is that it is a tiny percentage. The more typical experience is short-lived and not profitable for the women. And that is before you get to the question of what the experience of performing in pornography is like. That roughly mimics prostitution. Not only are there disproportionally high rates of drug and alcohol abuse but there are also disproportionately high rates of women in the industry with histories of sexual trauma, most likely childhood trauma, and that often these are women without a lot of other life choices. So when people say to me women choose this, they get paid, they consent, I say yeah that is true enough, everyone consents in some case to everything they do short of getting thrown in prison or something. The real question is not do we choose but what are the conditions under which we choose? If you are 18 years old and a high school dropout with a history of sexual trauma, and no marketable work skills then what does it mean to say you choose; well you choose at some level, I don't want to say people don't have agency. But as I always tell students, everybody chooses under conditions of some constraint and some opportunity. The question is how do we determine the constraints and opportunities under which people make choices."

Dr. Jensen elaborated on this point,

"A legal writer who is cited in my book, she was talking about it in the context of prostitution, when men buy women through prostitution, they never know the conditions under which that woman chose. And so every time you do that, you are in a sense exploiting; you are making a choice as a man to purchase a woman with no knowledge of the choices under which she made that choice. I think the same thing is true for pornography. When guys say a woman in pornography has a choice and they pick a dvd off the shelf or click on a link, they have no way of knowing the choices or conditions under which that woman chose. Given the clear patterns of women under conditions of great constraint, then it is the man's choice that is much more interesting. Because men can easily choose not to click on the link or not to buy the dvd. So we tend to focus on women's choices to perform in pornography and we tend to ignore the fact that men are choosing as well and men know more about the nature of the choice they are making than they portend."

A Performer's Experience

Have you ever talked with someone who appeared in pornography? Until I spoke with January Villarubia, I hadn't. I interviewed Ms. Villarubia recently and asked her to tell her story, so that you the reader can better understand what leads people to go into the pornography industry and what the reality is like. I report what she told me at length, below.

"It started for me when I was a child. What a lot of people don't understand is that most women who get into porn, it's not like they are little girls dreaming of becoming a porn star one day. And most of the women who get into the porn industry have come from a history of child abuse in one way or another. That was pretty much my story. I was basically raped in a broken home. My parents divorced when I was 3 years old. My mom had full custody of my sister and I; we grew up in a rough part of the inner city of Chicago so I had a lot of bad influences on me. My dad was kind of like a weekend dad at best, so I really didn't have that positive male influence in my life. Even though my mother did raise us in church, I really didn't have an idea about who God was. At the age of 5 years old, my mom met a European man who started to take her on long trips to Europe. At that time she would leave us with family members, whoever would take us in, so we weren't close to her side of the family but she would have to leave us with them so she could go on these long extended trips to Europe.

January described her experience staying with one of the families she was left with as a child.

"(They) had 2 children – one was a girl, one a boy. (The girl) was 4 years my senior. So by the age of 10 years old, my mom had gone on another one of these trips, it was a year or a year and a half. Most of her trips before then had been for 4-6 months. She would go back and forth. So it was a good environment for us up until that point. We loved going to (this family's) house, we had fun there, we enjoyed their house more than any other relatives that she would leave us with."

When January's mother would go away, that is when the sexual abuse started.

> "One night (the daughter) came to me and started talking about love and relationships and sex and as a little girl I had no idea what she was talking about but I was very intrigued because I had a hole in my heart already from not really having love or experiencing it in any kind of way. So conversations after a while turned into touching and so basically my first sexual experience was by (the daughter) at the age of 10 years old, she molested me, she was 14 at the time. And so you know she swore me to secrecy because after the first experience I was very upset but she said, 'Don't tell anybody, its ok, this is just what you do when you are alone with someone.'"

This first experience was difficult for January to move past, particularly because the abuse continued. She noted

> "So, that went on for a period of 2 years and I became very promiscuous because obviously that is going to mess with a little girl's head. So I started being very flirtatious with boys and you know thinking ok I have it all figured out [she laughed] relationship-wise, because she has already schooled me on all of these things, so I've already been there sexually. I hadn't actually had sex with anybody at that point, and then I ended it with her at like 12-and-a-half years old. I said, 'This is it, I can't do

this anymore; we're not going to do this.' And so I never said anything about it, I never told my mom, my family, anybody."

Not telling anyone is typical of people who survive sexual violence, especially at a young age.[108] When January turned 13, her life got more chaotic.

"I was hanging out with a lot of rough crowds already going to a lot of inner-city parties, getting drunk and experimenting with pot and things like that. I met a neighborhood boy who I thought was really into me, really cared about me, told me all the things that I really wanted to hear and I believed him. I was still searching desperately for love to fill that void, so he convinced me to ditch school one day and go to his house and he said, 'I'm going to make this really romantic lunch for you and it is just going to be great.' Well, it was anything but that when I got to his house, he ended up raping me and taking my virginity and he made me swear, 'don't tell your mom, don't tell your family, I know where you live, I'm going to kill you, I'm going to come to your house, I'm affiliated with all these gangs.'"

January was in a devastatingly tough spot. The boy she thought really cared about her set her up, raped her, and threatened to kill her if she told anyone. So, she didn't.

"I knew he had gang members who were his best friends. And so I believed him, which is why I didn't tell anybody. And that just catapulted into promiscuous behavior. And at the age of 15 ... we are moving a lot, my mom had trouble keeping a place, a stable environment over our head, my dad was a weekend dad so I had that instability, I didn't have anyone to go to talk to, my mom was really independent, handle this on your own, everything was 'do this on your own, you don't need anybody.'

January described getting into a relationship with a boy who himself had been sexually abused. She figured that if she showed him love, he would do the same for her and give her everything she was missing. They became sexually active and continued a tumultuous relationship. Later, January began having children. She worked to support her children, did so while going back to school, and attempted to provide for her family. She found herself in a situation where she was running out of money to feed her baby and she became desperate.

"I just started looking for a way to make extra money. So I opened up the yellow pages and I started looking, 'What can I do!?' I saw this section of 20-25 pages for escorts. I said, 'I've heard about this, I can be Julia Roberts. I can be pretty woman. I can go on a date with a rich guy and be paid for it.' I kind of knew what the reality of escorting was but I didn't really know the reality, what to expect, that sex was definitely expected and all of these things. So I did one randomly, made a phone call, the madam seemed very inviting, very nice, she said, 'Yeah come down, we will talk.'"

Against her better instincts, January went to talk with the madam.

"I met her and she just fell in love with how young I was, and she said, 'We can sell you so many different ways' and she said, "We are going to put you to work tonight.' So I asked, 'What does that mean exactly?' She didn't explain; she just basically threw a bunch of condoms at me and said, 'go to work.' At that point, I became a prostitute ... Through all of this I am still trying to go back to school, I am still working legitimately off and on. It was just crazy."

January's life got even more complicated and further from God as time went on. She married, divorced, and had three children.

I was doing what I had to do; I was working legitimately. I was working two full time jobs actually, trying to go back to school. I was always trying to go back to school. And, in 2006, I just found myself in a situation where I was about to lose our apartment, I wasn't making ends meet, I was a nervous wreck, had no support system, I wasn't in church, and I went looking for ways to make extra money."

January chose the only way she could figure out how to keep her children from being homeless.

"This time I went online and I went on Craigslist. At that time, they had an adult section. Basically. I went there and I saw an ad asking for BBW models, which is big beautiful women, since I had done some plus sized modeling before, I figured I could do this. So I went to the apartment, which was here in Las Vegas, and got there and there were two guys there and I'm like, 'OK, this is a little shady but I need this money right now.' So I went in the apartment, they took a few pictures of me, and then the guys were like, 'we need you to get undressed.'

So I said, "Like, what do you mean?' He was like, 'Well, we took the pictures but we really need you to do this scene.' And I said, 'What scene, what are you talking about?' And he was like, 'We need you to get undressed, we need you to have sex with us, and we need you to play with these toys on camera.'"

What she thought was a reasonably safe and mundane photo shoot turned out to be a situation where she was being cast in a pornographic film. And she was desperate for money because she was about to be kicked out of her apartment onto the street with her three children.

"Yeah, I was completely taken aback. I didn't know what to say at that point. Should I run, what should I do? I was between a rock and a hard place. So I did the scene and they made me sign a contract in legal terms that I didn't understand, I had no idea what it said, but they said this is part of it, so you have to sign it or we are not going to pay you. So I did it, they paid me $300; as I was leaving they were ushering another girl in. I felt sick to my stomach, I was like, 'I'm never going to do this again!' My God this was a horrible experience but I was able to feed my kids and that is all I cared about and I was able to pay some bills."

January hoped that would be the end. It wasn't.

"So, six months down the line, same situation, I am just hard up for money … … a couple of friends who had seen my first video, because what a lot of women who naively go into these things, once you sign the paper, you have lost privileges for life, they can do whatever they want to those images and that scene

and there is nothing you can ever do about it. So I
didn't know it was going to be out there for the entire
world to see like that, so, they were like, 'Why don't
you just go back into porn, it is a good way to make
extra money.' You cannot worry about it; they made
it seem like such a great life. So, after thinking about
it for awhile, I was like, 'I feel like I have no choice
right now and I was just desperate enough to do it.'"

As January sunk deeper into the world of porn, she felt worse and worse.

"So I put out an ad on an adult website and then
literally after I put out the ad I had calls within 5
minutes. They just ranged from like really strange
and obscene to outright crazy. I had a guy ask me if
I would sleep with a 14-year-old boy. I had people
asking me if I would do stuff with animals, I mean
it was just crazy. So, of course, I hung up on those
calls right away. I did sift through the ones that I
thought could be legitimate. ... I had nobody that
was going to be there for me to say, 'You are about
to enter a very dangerous industry, let me really
break this down for you.' But all of these producers
and agents were like, 'Come here, come there. So I
went out to California and I started doing porn. I
was in the porn industry for about a year and a half,
almost 2 years before I was at a point where I had
completely lost all identity and the whole reason I
was in the porn industry was for my children, to
support my children, but I had nothing to show for
my time in porn except for disease, more heartache,
and I was ready to kill myself. So, it was a horrible,
tragic experience. A lot of bad things happened
while I was in the industry. That is what brought

me to the point of wanting to end it all. I searched for help and that is how I found Shelley Lubben (from the nonprofit organization, The Pink Cross)."

At the breaking point and seconds from committing suicide, January reached out for help.

"At the point of wanting to take my life, I had a bottle of alcohol and pills in front of me, and the computer. And I had been crying and praying and said, 'OK, Lord, give me a solution or I'm taking myself out of this equation. I'm done.' So, after four hours of tearful crying and praying, I got online and searched "porn help" and Shelley's name popped up right away. She immediately responded to my email; she asked me what my situation was, how she could help. I started telling her about my kids, that I was in a very bad living situation. She immediately started sending me not only resources and referrals in my area to try to help me out, but also gift cards and, you know, support financially to help me pay my rent and make sure that the kids had food and she basically went to bat for me. I told her I was still receiving threats from the porn industry, from my previous web designer, and all of these scenes. Shelley said, 'Don't worry, we are going to send him a cease and desist letter.' She just went through all of these things immediately to stick up for me so it was great and, you know, I've been working with her ever since to basically bring light to the negative side of the porn industry, what happens behind the scenes to these girls."

January finally found her way out of the worst of all situations. I asked her to tell me more about the people she met in the pornography industry.

> "What most people don't understand, they are coming from these histories already where they have low self esteem, they have little self worth, they have been victimized their entire life. I'm not saying every one, but the majority of girls that I know personally and I have talked to come from these types of backgrounds, and so this is all they know and this is all they believe they are worth. So once they get into the industry, the porn producers feed off of that, they add on top of that, and they are constantly forcing them to do parts of scenes and acts that they never agreed to do, plus they are using things like drugs and alcohol to keep them submissive … They are going to be dominant over you and they are going to do whatever they have to do to keep you submissive, they just get you to do what they want you to do."

January spoke at length about being rescued from the industry by Shelley Lubben from Pink Cross.

> "So I know for a fact that He put her in my life. Shelley is a guardian angel to me. She wasn't just giving lip service, she came to my house and met me and my children, she brought gifts for my kids, and she nurtured me back into a relationship with the Lord and wanted to make sure that I was ok. She has gotten so much flack from both the church and the porn industry. … So, you know, she has really put her life on the line, and her family's life on the line, to be an advocate for these women. What it

really comes down to, being there to protect them, and of course the porn industry distorts what we do and tries to make it like we are against them. We want to make sure that you [women in the pornography industry] are protected, that you are safe, and that you realize that you can do so much more in life, so it is really pulling out the treasure in these women and helping them see that."

When January mentioned that they were putting their lives on the line, I asked her to elaborate.

"We have received death threats, her [Shelley Lubben's] family has quite often, actually a lot more than I have. I have, oh yeah. We have literally been stopped when we have tried to enter a porn convention and they told security, we have to reposition you because we have received death threats and we think they are going to actually act on it. People have sent things to her house with distorted images of her children, it is crazy so I just see her suffer so much and it is all because she truly loves these people. She runs a nonprofit, her and her husband have given so much of their own finances to make this happen, so it is just you have to have a heart for people who do this and that is what a lot of these women and men need, we are here for them. We feel like we understand what they have lost and what they are losing."

I asked January what she would say to an 18-year-old young man who told her that it is okay to use pornography because it is free and he isn't hurting anybody. Her response was quick and certain.

"First of all that is not true, because porn drives up the demand for sex trafficking and they have commercialized the exploitation that comes with it. It drives up the demand, also, in the things in your mind that it is okay to do these acts to women. That is unnatural. People are being paid, first of all, they are not happy to do it, why would you want to try to clean up something that ... once you have learned how rampant STIs are you really get turned off to it. What you see is this tiny, 30-minute package that has been cut and edited in so many ways. What you see is this whole fantasy and that is what they are feeding society. A lot of these girls who are trafficked are forced to watch pornography so that they know how to satisfy their customers, you know, their buyers. On top of that, a lot of these girls who are in sex trafficking are actually forced to do those pornographic films. So, the porn producers will get these girls to say that they are not under the influence of drugs or alcohol and that they are at least 18 years of age, but that is not the case! A lot of these girls are as young as 13 or 14 years old. See that is the thing, though. All they are doing is getting these girls to say that they are 18. A lot of the time they are supposed to keep copies of their IDs but there is nobody policing the porn industry."

I asked January what someone could do to help. She replied,

"The biggest way to tackle it is to make sure you are not watching it, and if you know people who are watching it, there are so many resources out there with factual things about what goes on behind the scenes. Not just Pink Cross (www.thepinkcross.org)

but also the National Center on Sexual Exploitation (http://endsexualexploitation.org) and Covenant Eyes (www.covenanteyes.com). Fight the New Drug (www.fightthenewdrug.org) is great, it talks about how porn affects brain chemistry. Porn is very much an addiction and it affects your brain chemistry because it artificially stimulates you. There are so many resources, once you've learned the truth, it is hard to walk away from that. If you do have a hardcore addiction, it may be harder for you opposed to someone messing around with it. I think, when it comes to the consumer, there are a lot of people who watch porn because they believe that these girls love what they do. We don't love what we do! We are paid to lie to every camera and so it leads to the idea that we like you. We don't like you, especially once we are in the industry, we are drugged out of our mind. We hate men, period. Because of everything that is done on set and off set, because for most women in the porn industry, they don't have stable relationships while they are in the industry. We are not there to please you or satisfy you, we don't care. We are there to make money. We are not enjoying any part or any aspect of what we are doing. Porn is not glamorous in any sense."

A Closing Thought

The content we have discussed in this chapter, now in the mainstream, is terribly harmful. In my interview with Dr. Paul Wright of Indiana University, he noted

"Mainstream content – in other words, the content that is most popular and commonly consumed – is definitely doing more harm than good – I don't think there is any doubt about that."

As confirmation of that effect, we need only look at what the pornography industry says itself about its intent. When Dr. Robert Jensen attended a convention for the pornography industry, he asked a producer there what he tries to show people through his movies. The producer responded,

> "I'd like to show what I believe the men want to see: violence against women. I firmly believe that we serve a purpose by showing that."[109] (p. 70).

Chapter 7

Women's Use of Pornography

This chapter highlights the research, scholarly perspectives, and anecdotes about how, when, and why women use pornography. Perhaps you are reading this and thinking, "I'm a woman, I don't view pornography, I grew up in a Christian home, I live with a Christian family, this doesn't affect me." Not so. Abundant research shows that pornography affects today's culture, in which we all live. Pornography has profound effects on how women are expected to behave sexually, encouraging that they accept sexual violence. In addition, Internet pornography tends to depict the opposite of what most seek in a marriage – disrespect, promiscuity, detachment, and abuse.[110] As philosopher Dr. Rebecca Whisnant has written, today's mainstream pornography places hostile and humiliating acts toward women front and center.[111]

Women view pornography less frequently than men.[112] [113] [114] That is a surprise to no one. Relative to men, women have their first experience seeing pornography later, watch porn less frequently, are more likely to use pornography with their current sexual partner, and are less likely to view pornography alone. Women also tend to prefer soft-core pornography over the hardcore porn preferred by men.[115] In my interview with Dr. Gail Dines, she observed, "women are not looking at the same thing. What their boyfriends show them is the milder kind, which is hard to find. They do it to groom them into porn sex."

Most studies (as opposed to presumably inflated porn industry reports) have found that about one-third of young women view pornography. A 2008 study found that 31% of college-age women use pornography.[116] A study of U.S. women nationwide conducted by a research team led by Dr. Paul Wright of Indiana University found that before the Internet, when women's pornography use was measured, rates varied a great deal from year to year. After the Internet was introduced in the 1990s, women's overall use rose slightly and remained more stable year-to-year. For women age 18-30, approximately 34% view pornography at least once a year.[117]

Political Beliefs

Another of Dr. Wright's findings from his 2013 study was that pornography use was more likely among women who were younger, less religious, and non-white. Women porn users more strongly believed that sex outside of an established marriage was acceptable, and more strongly supported premarital sex among both adults and teenagers. Women porn users had more sexual partners in the last year as well as in the last five years; furthermore, they were also more likely to have sex outside of marriage and have sex for money. In a more complex analysis, Dr. Wright and his colleagues found that the relationships between pornography use and risky sexual behavior was strongest for people who identified as politically liberal. The relationship between pornography use and risky sexual behavior were not very strong, or even nonexistent, for women who were politically conservative.[118]

Body Image

Dr. Ana Bridges, whose research I introduced earlier, worked with Drs. Chyng Sun, Matt Ezzel, and Jennifer Johnson in a study trying to tease out how pornography affects women's body image.[119] In a complex study, their preliminary results show that women's body image is affected by pornography, but in a complicated way. The more women use pornography, the more likely they are to act in ways that are consistent with pornography in their own sexual encounters. And the more women act like females in pornography movies, the lower their self esteem, the lower their bodily self image, and the less they are satisfied with their relationship. The effects of pornography, for women, travel through the route of their behavior during sexual encounters to reach a destination of unhappiness.

Katie, whom we met earlier, mentioned such body image issues. She reported,

> "they say guys want girls that are perfectly thin, the perfect body, in high school we were all like, 'We can't eat that' [an expression of wanting to be thin based on what women see in pornography] But I think it mentally affects you like your body image, the way you see yourself when you are growing up. I know it exists and men look at it and as a woman it makes you think, 'Well, I guess I'm not what they want so I think that is why women do that [weight control].'"

Seeing pornography, particularly on a secular college campus, is a common experience for women.[120] For example, Makynlee is an African-American, married woman in her 30s. She takes a passive approach to life, saying "whatever" as a mantra. Her frequent nervous laughter is pronounced. She recounted seeing pornography during her first year of college.

"I just remember my first year in college, we would, like, chill out in the dorms and say, like, 'Well we're bored, oh, like, so-and-so has this porn let's see what it is [laughs].' And we'd laugh and critique it and find out things [laughs]."

Selling Out

When I interviewed philosophy professor Dr. Rebecca Whisnant and asked her what she thought women should keep in mind when deciding whether or not to look at pornography, she noted,

"I think there are important points to be made about owning and controlling your sexuality and not putting such an intimate and important part of yourself up for sale. So as a porn consumer you are essentially saying 'here is this very intimate very vulnerable part of myself and I'm going to put it in the hands of pimps. I'm going to let pimps shape me to find certain things sexually pleasurable.' That deprives them of the opportunity to develop their own authentic sexuality in the context of their own relationships with themselves and/or others. I think that is really important, and once you have done that [use pornography] it is really hard to undo it."

One participant I spoke with who seems to fit the mold Dr. Whisnant described of putting her sexuality up for sale was Sarah, whom we met earlier. She noted that she began looking at pornography when she was 7.

"I did investigate it more when I was growing up, like in high school I started watching some pornography, I would watch, like, little clips of it, so

> I did kind of, like, explore my curiosity. So I guess that started around the same time, like craving attention from guys and watching pornography around age 13ish." She continued, "More of it has to do with curiosity. I have this, like, I wonder what that is like, so then I see it and then the curiosity goes away. I don't want to keep watching most of the things …"

When I asked her if she ever tried to cut down her pornography use, she replied "Yeah, so, like, when I was in high school, I used to watch pornography multiple times a week. So now, it is like maybe once a week, maybe, if that. I did watch it a lot more in high school and stuff and I'm not as sexually frustrated now, so I don't watch it as often."

Antisocial Personalities

Another line of research has examined whether people who use pornography more frequently also have some characteristics of mental illness. For example, Dr. Bryant Paul of Indiana University found that heavy users of pornography – both men and women – are also more likely to have psychopathic, antisocial personalities.[121] An example of antisocial behavior being associated with pornography use is in the life experience of Katie, particularly with a group of male friends she had in college. She described many instances where a group of guy friends of hers would show her pornography when she didn't want to see it.

> "When I was like 20, the 'Farm Guys' were always playing jokes on the field hockey girls. One of them sent us a link saying 'This is the most funniest video ever' and it was like a (porn scene with several people together). Yeah, so we all pull it up and are

like 'What!!' So we think we have the wrong link but we didn't. They were just trying to be stupid and funny but it is not really funny to girls. To guys it is funny because you got us to watch a scene of a porn. Maturity I guess." When I asked her what she thought the Farm Guys intended to do, she said, "I have no idea, because that was really weird. Maybe to make us think that it is OK for them to (do that) with us or something ... All of us kind of looked at each other and said, 'Do they think we were going to do that?' Maybe there was an intention to do that. I think they were kinda testing the waters to do that."

A particularly disturbing kind of anti-social behavior characterized the Farm Guys. Katie noted that the Farm Guys would let their guy friends watch their live sexual encounters.

"They did some weird things, if they brought a girl into their dorm, they would purposely leave the door cracked so it would come open when they were having sex with the girl. As a girl, I would say something. I was like, 'Are you wanting everyone to see this happen?' Sometimes I think it is an ego thing at the age of a 20 year old guy, 'Guys would literally walk by and say, 'Yeah man, like, you got another one!' Like they are counting or something, like it is a game to them. I know they were counting. 'Yeah, I got 8!' One of them [girls] actually got really mad, said get off me, hit him, and she walked out. Some of them are too embarrassed to even fight it so they just hide their face."

Viewing to please a man

The most common reason that women cite for viewing pornography is to please a sexual partner.[122] While interviewing women for this book, I discovered that many participants had this experience, where their boyfriend asked them to view pornography. For example, "Ella" is a woman who we met in chapter four. Her boyfriend asked her to watch pornography.

> "He asked if I wanted to watch it, I said, 'OK, sure,' and we sat on my bed and watched it. It was gross. I realized that it just wasn't something for me, and that is what spiraled our relationship going down. I was like, 'Why do you have to watch this and what is this doing for you because it is not doing anything for me so why do you have to watch it?' It was harmful to the relationship."

Ella first saw pornography at age 11. She notes,

> "It was weird because this is when the Internet started to take off so when you would click on a website it would take you to a porn site. You wouldn't mean to click on it, but these ads would always pop up. One day I was at home by myself on my computer and that happened [a pop up] as I was doing my homework and it happened and I was like, 'I want to look and see,' so I clicked on it and it took me to a pornography site and it was the first time I saw that. I learned that it is addicting because, I didn't become addicted to it but it was intriguing so I would come home after school wanting to look at more of it, and at this time, I was a part of a Christian organization at

school. I realized that it was just more than naked people, it was messing with my mind at 11, I felt shame, guilt, I felt disgusting, and I realized then and there that it is not something to be played with and it has serious consequences."

Ella continued to look at pornography off and on until she was pregnant at 21. She recalled this experience

"One experience I had, I was up late at night because when you are pregnant you can't really sleep, 6-7 months in, I saw this porn video on HBO so I was like, 'Well, my boyfriend is not here … so I watched it, I got disgusted afterward. I was like, 'I can't do this with a child in me, I cannot do this period,' like the guilt and the shame that came afterward was tremendous and I was just like, 'No, never again,' and I haven't looked at it ever since."

Another participant who was shown pornography by a male friend was Taylor, a woman in her 30s from Thailand, who is temporarily visiting the United States to advance a business career. She is short with lively eyes and a cheerful spirit. She identifies as Buddhist. She remembers well the first time she saw a pornographic picture.

"When I was in college, my friend is like, he brought out a Japanese (pornographic) magazine and said, 'Hey, look at this, look at these beautiful ladies, they are beautiful in the body.' I was like, 'That was insane. Hey dude, why did you show me this picture?' He was like, 'Why, she is beautiful, they are beautiful.' I think he just wanted to show off, well he knows these girls, this girl is beautiful."

Katie was also shown pornography by a man. Katie noted that she sees pornography about once a month, mostly in a way that is unintentional.

> "It is just kind of out there. I feel like you type in the wrong thing in a computer and it pops up, you are not even meaning that. Yeah, about once a month would be the most. I mean if you are around school on campus and stuff, people literally just have it on their phones and they are not trying to hide it – men and women, just depends, it's usually around night time, classes are out. If I'm going to go study in the library sometimes people have it up on their own laptop. It is kind of weird, why would you do that in public? I'm not going to, like, sit there and watch it with them. It is odd to me that they are that comfortable to do that. They are sometimes like, 'Hey this video is hilarious, go watch it!' And it comes up and they are just being stupid [showing me porn].

A potential harm in women viewing pornography can be a decreased ability to detect a violent man. For example, a research team at the University of Washington led by Dr. Kelly Davis looked into whether women evaluate violent pornographic images differently based on whether they have consumed a moderate amount of alcohol or not. They found that alcohol consuming participants were less likely to label a movie they viewed in which a rape occurred as "rape" than sober participants. Under the influence of alcohol, women developed more calloused attitudes toward rape and rape victims. Though rape is of course never the fault of someone who survives it, it is reasonable to bear in mind that pornography is associated with increased risk, particularly when someone is under the influence of alcohol.[123]

A Concluding Thought

Generally speaking, the research and experiences shared in this chapter indicate that women's use of pornography is often either an unintentional experience or one that is encouraged by a man. Sometimes it is to satisfy curiosity. Regardless, the impact of viewing pornography tends to result in some sort of harm for the viewer – in their body image, relationship quality, or their mental health. And without question, the spiritual consequences of indulging in the desires of the flesh and of the eyes leads people away from the Father (1 John 2:16, ESV).

Chapter 8

Impact on Youth and Teenagers

The youth and teen years are highly impressionable. During this time, people develop their understanding of sexual relations, establish their identity, and begin to establish the ability to delay gratification.[124] [125] When high doses of pornography are injected into this time, the scripts that are encoded in a brain can become foundational events that stay with the person.[126] [127]

Jennifer first saw pornography at the age of 4. Though the age at which she saw it is earlier than average, the way she ran into it is quite common. The impact was devastating. She was the first person who walked through my office door volunteering to participate in the study for this book.

Jennifer is a Native American mother of two in her 20s, who is working her way through school. Seeing pornography at the age of 4 was deeply unsettling. She describes this experience,

> "It was uncomfortable. It kind of made me question what was going on because I didn't quite understand. I always thought it was wrong, I shouldn't be seeing this; I would run away. I think that I thought that I would get in trouble if I saw it." I asked her if pornography

affected her in any particular way. I found her response chilling, "It definitely affected me. I grew up in a very abusive home and I was taken out of that home by DHS at the age of 11 and so was my older sister, younger sister, and younger brother. I had two older sisters. One was a teen mom and the other ended up in [juvenile detention] at a young age. And I think it affected them big time. There was also a lot of sexual abuse going on in the house. I didn't know about it but one of my sisters informed me. A lot of the sexual abuse was from the pornography that my brother was watching. He was influenced by it because that is all he knew. We were pretty much kept in the house; we weren't allowed to go anywhere so all we were exposed to was each other. So I think at his age in the changes that he was going through in puberty, with the influence of pornography that definitely made an impact on the way that he viewed sex and the way he viewed my sisters and anybody else in the home."

I asked if Jennifer would say more about the sexual abuse. She said,

"My brother was sexually abusing my sister. I think they found the [pornographic] tape from my biological parents and cause there was also drug abuse going on, while they (my parents) were tending to their habits, my brother and sister were tending to their other habits. And I do remember when I was 5, I walked in and they (my 9 year old brother and 7 year old sister) were watching pornography and they were performing sexual acts on each other. And being a 5 year old that scared me so I kind of just left the room and didn't know what to think, but I knew it was bad. So at a very young age I knew what sex was."

When Exposure Typically Begins

In the United States, people who are 18 years old or older are the only ones who can legally access pornography. The reality is that most people, especially boys, see pornography well before turning 18. And they are seeing it at younger and younger ages. Between 2008 and 2011, exposure to porn among boys under the age of 13 jumped from 14% to 49%. Daily use among this group more than doubled[128]. Before teens get to college, 93% of boys and 62% of girls have seen online pornography. The circumstances surrounding viewing pornography tend to differ based on whether one is a boy or a girl. Boys tend to seek it out while much of the exposure girls have is unwanted – having it shown to them by others.[129] Most young people age 18 to 24 view pornography as just another acceptable practice in life. In fact, two thirds (67%) of young men and one half (49%) of young women agree that viewing pornography is acceptable.[130]

Dr. William Struthers is a Professor of Psychology at Wheaton College and the author of *Wired for Intimacy: How Pornography Hijacks the Male Brain.*[131] In my recent interview with Dr. Struthers, I asked him what effect pornography has on children. He noted,

> "It provides the script by which they think a sexual encounter should be following … … so it creates that script by which they think that is supposed to be how an encounter goes." He continued, "My concern is that it is doing a couple things. It is rare that pornography has clear consent that is tied to it, so you see it is just implied and it is very narrow. They are beginning to be more segmented in how they think about sexual acts; that they are separate from a larger relational context." Dr. Struthers also notes that pornography use tends to lead to risky sexual acts and to the abuse of substances during a sexual encounter.

Dr. Kevin Skinner is a therapist who counsels teens addicted to pornography. He notes that most begin their involvement with pornography between ages 10 and 14. He further reports that parents of porn addicted teens tend to be either very rigid and controlling or completely disinterested and disengaged. Teens with controlling parents tend to experience shame, which lead them to behaviors they find comforting to lessen the feeling of rejection by their parents. He further notes that addiction is a likely result for kids who use pornography and are either isolated or feel lonely.[132]

In a study of early adolescent use of pornography, two thirds of boys and one third of the girls had seen sexually explicit media during the last year. Those whose parents were less educated and those who were higher on sensation seeking were more likely to have viewed pornography. Boys who viewed pornography at an earlier age than average were more likely to have sexually harassed a peer.[133]

Girls' Initial Experiences

Several of the women I interviewed for this study mentioned their recent experience as teenagers who were shown pornography when they didn't want to see it. Whether an adolescent seeks pornography or not, coming face-to-face with it is likely. Well over two-thirds of 15-17 year old adolescents have seen porn websites when they did not intend to access them.[134]

One woman I interviewed who talked about her experience as a girl seeing pornography was Sarah. Sarah is a 19-year-old female, Caucasian sophomore in college who is relatively unconnected to her campus and is not particularly involved in a faith community. Sarah discussed a time when she saw pornography at age 7.

> "When I was younger, my parents and my aunts didn't have a lot of money so we lived with my

grandma. So, I grew up with a bunch of boy cousins and so they had a video of pornography and I went to go get them for dinner and it was, like, on in there and I knew that they watched it. I guess I was like 7, and they were like 8 and 13 … It was kinda weird to me at first; I mean, I was always like a good little kid, I was kind of curious about it but I wasn't going to, like, look into it further; I knew it was something that I wasn't supposed to look at until I was older, if at all."

Kaitlin, a 19-year-old college sophomore, reported that friends in high school sent her pornographic pictures, frequently. Describing what she was sent, she recalls,

"My friends would joke around and send like gross [pornographic] stuff. Like, my friends would send gross videos, whatever is going around school. I was grossed out, like, 'eww!' My friends do it to this day, and I'm like, 'I don't want any part of it.'" She still receives such videos once or twice a month.

Boys' Initial Experiences

Boys also experience unwanted viewing of pornography. Paul, a Christian young man who we met in earlier, told me that his addiction to pornography started when friends insisted on showing it to him in order to embarrass him when he was 14.

"They would be like joking around like, 'Look at this.' They'd pull up some porn video on their iPhone. My freshman year was, like, a big exposure because I was kept pretty innocent and, like, guarded from being exposed to sexual images on TVs and all that stuff, we don't have cable and stuff like that, and so in the football locker room itself when guys would talk about stuff I wouldn't know what they were talking about and they would go 'Hey Paul, what do you think about that?' I'd say 'I don't really know.' I would be known as 'the virgin' and stuff like that, and I remember one time a guy after practice thought it was ridiculous that I had never seen porn so he would show it to me, and I'd be like, 'I don't know about that.' I was waiting for my mom to pick me up, and he would look something up and say 'Hey, look at this.' I just looked away and said, 'Yeah, ok, whatever.' He was in unbelief that I wouldn't want to look at it." Paul described his developing addiction. "I mean, from 15 probably to 17 it was pretty much 3-4 days a week, it started like every so often but as time progressed, every time I masturbated with it. It would go on in bathrooms when I got home from school, I would directly go to a bathroom ..."

Another male who had a similar experience was Henry, an overweight, socially awkward Hispanic college student. He recalls friends who made him

"see some really strange things every once in a while. Like, a friend will pop up something really weird some sort of fetish 'how ridiculous is this ... ... I was like 'why are you showing me this ... ... how much pain can she actually take?"

One reason that boys show other boys pornography seems to be due to a right of passage ritual. For example, Sam spoke of his early experiences with pornography, and how his peers influenced each other.

> "Honestly, I didn't really comprehend it at first, I just kind of watched it, at the time, you weren't cool if you hadn't seen porn yet. It was just kinda like a social thing where you just kinda do stuff like that to kinda fit in. At a certain age you are expected to know certain things and see certain things. It was like an unwritten law that, like, the older brother would show the younger brother and he would show his friend and it's kinda being in a clique; you just had to know. If you didn't see it, well, they would probably show you just to show you and you kinda just move on."

When I asked Dr. Walter DeKeseredy what his research shows about the pornography consumption of teenage boys, he noted

> "It is an integral part of leisure activities. Those who are not consuming are seen as deviant. There is significant peer pressure; there are people who don't like it, for whatever reason. There is substantial amount of pressure to consume it. The thing that is also interesting is the misogyny that is coming out. When these guys view it together, the misogyny is absolutely incredible, the way they talk to the screens and all of that. It is an integral part of peer groups. Those who resist are at the margins."

Jack, a man I interviewed for this book whom we met before, described a time during college when he watched pornography with guys in his fraternity.

"We always joked around about it, we'd go on trips and we'd stop off at the store on the way, I call them smut stores ... ... as a whole group we all went on a big bus trip and they had a VCR and we picked up a movie and watched it, harmless type stuff, it was just joking around and watching it kind of stuff. We were all drinking and eating and whatever was playing in there. It was pornography. Not everyone on the bus was into it; it was just playing. Usually one of the brothers was doing color commentary of it. Just jokin' around."

I asked Jack to describe more about what he and his friends would joke about when watching pornography. He responded,

"Making fun of the man's (private parts) ... ... You'd always have one person who would describe the technique as if it is a sporting event. You always have some guy making fun of the video quality, how cheaply it is made."

I found this pattern of behavior interesting, so I asked Jack to talk about how laughing at a pornography film would change if women were there. He eagerly responded,

"pretty much the same things, you'd hear more jokes from the women, guys would look at the girls and say 'why don't you do that kind of stuff' (in reference to the pornographic movie). She would look at the guys and say 'if you are like that, then I would.' You know, those type of jokes. You'd see more joking between each other as much as they are making fun of what is on TV."

Another participant, John, described this use of pornography in peer groups. John described a typical experience of many males when they are young.[135]

> "When I was younger, in 7th or 8th grade, I'd spend the night with friends, their older brother would have magazines so we would sneak into his room to look at them. I knew if I spent the night, I'd get a chance to look. My parents wouldn't know. They would not have suspected it if they knew the kids or the parents."

Indeed, young people will often go to great lengths to conceal their pornography use from their parents. For example, Sam described how he would go about looking at pornography when his parents were home.

> "I'd wait until my parents went to bed, wait a couple hours, and had the door so my parents couldn't see the lights (under the door); I put pillows under the door."

Like many males who view pornography, Greg started viewing at a young age. Now nearly age 30, he is on the cutting edge of the first generation with unlimited online access to online pornography. He has been actively fighting a porn addiction for about a decade. He first saw porn at age 9 when a friend wondered aloud if a store they were in had any porn. He hadn't heard the word before, so when he got home he typed it into the Internet to see what it meant. He recalls,

> "Pictures came up and it was terrifying and fascinating. I did that a couple more times and I knew I would get in huge trouble if it happened; I

knew it was bad. And then I got caught. They saw on the Internet history and so my Mom talked to me and I think I told her it was a pop up. That was kind of it. I remember my summer after 7th grade I discovered that I could download pictures on a music downloading thing and I remember seeing the back of some dvd that was at my grandma's house that had a woman in a bathing suit and that was the first of it. I realized you could download something and I did so all summer. I would just sneak around and download these pictures when my parents were gone. At the end of the summer, she saw some stuff on the history on the computer. She asked me about it and I said pop ups. They were going to church and leaving me at home; they told me not to get on the computer. 'Don't get on the computer, if you do, you are in trouble.' I was like 'Sure, I won't get on the computer.' They would leave, I would get on the computer and download pornographic pictures. When they got back, they looked at the history, they called me downstairs and I just remember my life was over. I was caught red handed. All of it was there. I lied. I just remember sitting there for a couple hours, just listening to them. My Mom was crying. I was crying. Just completely stunned. I was grounded for like 7 months and that was 8th grade and I didn't look at anything during that period. I was grounded from the computer, from video games; it turned out to be a blessing. I started playing a musical instrument; I started reading a lot."

Outside the U.S.

When pornography access has been studied in countries outside the U.S., early exposure is the typical finding. For example, among Italian high school students, over three-quarters have viewed pornography.[136] In Sweden, teen exposure to pornography is nearly universal, with boys seeking it out more than girls. Among the changes it seems to have produced include shaving genitals, for both boys and girls (a practice now also very common in the United States).[137] Many boys shave not only their genitals, but their entire bodies. Girls, in particular, were concerned that their bodies didn't measure up to the porn ideal.[138]

One of the participants I interviewed for this book, Taylor, is from Thailand. She attended a Thai high school and recounted a story she remembers well, "There was a guy, he came in front of my high school and he was, like, naked. My friend was really shocked. One of the teachers was there and he helped catch that guy and send him to the jail. He did that because he just watched a porn movie, it increased his need, I think, and he just tried to show off. That is what he told the police." She made a further observation about her home culture in Thailand, "A lot of kids right now record when they have sex and put it on the Internet because they want to show off; they want to be stars."

Generational Differences

Though today's generation of young people have more access to pornography than any generation before them, boys didn't just start looking at pornography when the Internet was created. In the 1980s, the average age a boy saw Playboy magazine was 11. By age 15, over 9 out of 10 had seen it. Of course, Playboy magazine depicted images that are far less violent than what exists in today's mainstream pornography, so much so that, in 2015, Playboy abandoned showing nude models as they couldn't compete with material online. However, even in the 1980s, by the time boys reached the 13-15 year old age range, 9 out of 10 had seen an X rated movie.[139]

Still, today's generation of children and adolescents have more access to pornography than any generation in the history of the world.[140] Sam summed this difference up well. Sam is a Caucasian male college student, who looks like a stereotypical fraternity guy with unwashed short hair and a ball cap he takes off and on repeatedly. He is fit, thin, and athletic. He grew up in a very progressive large city on the East Coast. He shared,

> "When I was a kid, I was never inside, I was always outside playing sports. Nowadays kids pretty much have an iPhone when they come out of the womb. The more technology you have in your possession the more opportunity you have, the more opportunity, the more likely you are [to look at porn]."

In my interview with Dr. DeKeseredy, we discussed how the average boy today was seeing pornography at age 11 and had essentially unrestricted access to it for all of his adolescence. I asked Dr. DeKeseredy what he thought the 11 year old boy of today would be like when he grew up, "He's going to be cruel, he's going to have unrealistic expectations, I think relationships are going to fall apart. I predict that divorce rates are going to increase significantly because of deep-rooted unhappiness."

Sexual Violence

One of the most disturbing impacts of young people's use of pornography is the influence it has on sexual violence. Much of the research on adolescents, pornography, and sexual violence shows that there is a portion of boys who are particularly susceptible to the violence-inducing effects of pornography. In a study examining the link between adolescent viewing of pornography and sexual assault, researchers found that for boys who are predisposed to be sexually aggressive, if they frequently consume pornography, they are four times more likely to commit sexual violence than their friends who infrequently use porn.[141] Later, members of the same research team extended this line of research. They followed a group of adolescents for 3 years, and found that those who intentionally viewed violent pornography were six times more likely to commit acts of sexual violence than those who did not view such pornography.[142]

The types of sexual violence committed by high risk boys was studied by a team of researchers including Dr. Eileen Alexy and Dr. Ann Burgess from Boston College and Dr. Robert Prentky from Farleigh Dickinson University. They studied children and adolescents who have a predisposition to sexually aggressive behavior. The researchers found that children and adolescents predisposed to sexual aggression who also use pornography are more likely to commit rape and are also more likely to have sex with animals than are similar juveniles who were not pornography consumers. Pornography consumers were also more likely to commit theft and arson.[143]

In a study that included both boys and girls, high and low risk adolescents, adolescents who viewed sexual explicit websites were almost three times more likely to have used alcohol or drugs during their last sexual experience (thus making sexual assault much more likely) and were twice as likely as other youth to have had anal sex.[144]

Seeing Women as Objects

The root of many acts of violence, including sexual violence, involves a process where an individual sees another person as more of an object than a human. To study this process, a research team in the Netherlands studied the relationship between adolescents looking at pornography and whether they believed women were objects, instead of people. They found that the more boys and girls viewed pornography, the more they believed that females *are* sex objects.[145] [146]

Bob, a 23-year-old athletic-looking Native American male college student I interviewed, describes this process of seeing women as objects. He believes that his use of pornography about every other day is an addiction. After I interviewed him, he told me that I was the only person with whom he has ever talked about his addiction. He first started looking at pornography at age 11 when his cousin was 15 and would put it on their television. His cousin watched at least once a day, often twice.

> "I tried to leave a lot because it was kinda strange, so in a week I'd watch it 2 or 3 times. It was, like, disgusting to me. It still is disgusting to me. It kind of affects me today. I don't like doin' it but I still, kind of, like, watch it. It is kinda like an addiction. Yeah. I pretty much watch it 2 or 3 times a week still since age 14."

Part of Bob's experience watching pornography at age 11 was atypical. While an older relative did introduce it to him (a typical experience), that is not all his relative showed him.

> "He masturbated right in front of me. It was strange. Then it made me curious because I was young and I was like, 'What is he doing' and everything and eventually, I started doing that, but usually not with him in the room. I wasn't, I was still young, so I was still shy and insecure about everything so I didn't want to be around him when it happened … … I thought it was gross, I didn't know what he was doing at the time. I don't really know how to

> explain in words how it felt at the time because I
> just can't, I can't remember what I was thinking
> or how I felt at the time because it made me really
> uncomfortable ..."

Bob reported that after the first time he saw pornography, he changed.

> "Vulgar thoughts happened to me the first time I
> saw it. I started thinking of women in a different
> way, as in sexual objects kind of. I see them as a
> sexual object like someone you want to have sex
> with, rather than someone you want to date."

Bob's experience helps to demonstrate how older boys can influence younger boys, and lead them in a direction that is away from the will of God and into behaviors that will undermine a healthy sexuality in the future.

Pornography and Young Brains

More and more research is being done on brain development, and how that relates to how adolescents and young adults are impacted by pornography. The impact of seeing pornography on a young person with a developing brain can be even more impactful than what is seen by an adult.[147] An adolescent brain has not yet fully matured, particularly in the control center for suppressing of anti-social sexual behaviors they see in pornography. Thus, adolescents may be particularly vulnerable to the impact of violent pornography and are at particular risk for acting on what they see.[148] [149]

Additional research on adolescent brains found that those who consume pornography are likely to believe things about sex that are unrealistic. Relatedly, girls who watch pornography report to researchers that they worry that their bodies don't look like the women in pornography. Boys express concern that they won't be able to perform as well as the men they see.[150]

Self-Recognition of Harm

Many of the participants I interviewed described habitual use of pornography to the point that they recognized it as harmful. For example, Tommy is an 18 year old college freshman, gangly and young looking with piercing blue eyes. He began looking at pornography at least weekly at the age of 13. He reported to me about a time when he was 15 when he was using pornography so frequently that he felt like he had to cut back.

> "There are times before I had a girlfriend that I kinda just keep going back to it and back to it. I think when you are younger you have more hormones than even now and it was just desire and you keep doing it and doing it and it kinda became almost painful because you can hurt yourself, soreness and just it's too much. Those times I was definitely like, 'Stop, back off, you don't want to do that again.' I wouldn't want to do it again because when I was doing it too much, next time you don't want to do it that much again. There was a time during a week when I'd do it 10 times during a week."

A Concluding Thought

Based on a comprehensive review of research articles on the impact of pornography on children, Dr. Paul Wright of Indiana University concluded that the viewing of pornography by children is widespread, and the more they view it, the more they do the often violent things they see in pornography.[151]

If you are concerned about the issues raised in this chapter, you may find some comfort in knowing that scholars are beginning to study what can inhibit the use of pornography by adolescents. One study found that adolescents who spend more time with friends in social situations are less likely to view pornography. Boys and girls who are less integrated into their religious group, school, family, and community consumed more pornography.[152] Thus, integration into these kinds of groups may help. In the coming years, more research will be conducted to explore the inhibiting factors of pornography use; I hope to report on those in a second edition of this book.

Chapter 9

Pro-Pornography Professors: The Academic Movement to Promote Violence Against Women

You might be asking why you should care about professors who are pro-porn. One reason is that those of us who are anti-porn need to understand the arguments of the other side in order to counter them. Pro-porn professors are particularly important to understand, because they speak with a sense of authority unlike many others. In my view, they are among the most insidious characters that collude with an industry bent on encouraging destroying that which God created and encouraging violence against women.

There are many arguments that academics and activists who support pornography attempt to weave together. However, upon inspection, the threads that bind them quickly unravel. Various individuals assert that pornography is empowering,[153] that it doesn't actually have the harmful effects supported by over 100 studies,[154] that it is consistent with feminist efforts to liberate women,[155] that it really isn't all that violent,[156] or that, on balance, it is just a great thing for society to have.[157] In this chapter, we will consider why these perspectives are not only in conflict with logic and reason, but also stand against the overwhelming weight of the scientific evidence.

In my own experience speaking about pornography at professional conferences, on college campuses, and in military environments, I've had many people challenge what I have to say about its real and potential harms. About a decade ago, a man in his 20s raised his hand at the end of a conference presentation I gave to about 100 college administrators and, with a combative tone, indicted me for being "sex negative." The label he attempted to brand me with was in opposition to his allegedly more desirable identity as "sex positive." I often find labels to be reductionist. This is a good example. Someone who is anti-porn is no more sex negative than food negative. Both sex and food have their place in the human experience. I can't think of an anti-porn person who would suggest eating 20,000 calories a day or would suggest consuming a bowl of spaghetti while walking on a high wire between two buildings. Those opinions don't make one food negative; just practical and healthy. In my case, I believe that there are certain boundaries that are appropriate for sexual intercourse (consensual relations in marriage between one man and one woman), but that doesn't make me sex negative. For example, I would suggest that sex is not advisable in the check-out line at a convenience store, it is not advisable with a 12-year-old, nor is it advisable with a close blood relative. Of course, many other good examples exist. The "sex negative" label is, like many other labels, one that a side of a contentious debate tries to pin on the other in an attempt to make them look ignorant. Today's culture is replete with examples. Like others in the anti-porn movement, I am not against sex. People in this movement tend to have a variety of opinions on appropriate contexts and conditions under which sexual behavior should be encouraged, discouraged, or be illegal. I certainly have mine. However, the anti-porn movement is united in its opposition to filming explicit sexual acts where men dominate women through sexualized violence.

Historically, two groups have been at the forefront of the anti-pornography movement, Christians and feminists. There are, of course, members of both groups who are also pro-porn. In this chapter, we will explore the perspective of people who are both pro- and anti-porn. Most of the people cited here take on the feminist label; though there is substantial disagreement in their perspectives.

The Basic Arguments

In my recent interview with Dr. Robert Jensen, whom we met in chapter 1, he described the two main types of academic pro-porn arguments. He asserted,

> "All of the pro-porn literature I see tends to be one of two things. Either it is this postmodern celebration of 'whatever,' heavily influenced by Queer Theory, where I can't make heads or tails of what they are even saying; it is academic word salad. Put words in a bowl, twirl them around, and however they land is fine. The other style of defense of porn I see in the academy is people who say, 'OK, I'll grant you that the bulk of the industry is misogynist and racist; what we really have to do is explore the frontiers. It is really about feminist porn.'"

Female Made and "Feminist" Pornography

Some contend that if women were in the director's chair of pornographic media, then the downsides of pornography would go away.[158] The argument is made that pornography is violent toward women because men make it. If women made it, it wouldn't be so problematic. As you may remember in Chapter 4, a group of researchers led by Dr. Chyng Sun from NYU studied whether having a female director versus a male director would impact the content in pornography. A statistical analysis of 122 randomly selected scenes from 44 top-renting adult videos (half male and half female-directed) found many more similarities than differences between pornography directed by men vs. women. In all films, both verbal and physical aggression was common. When one individual exercised aggression toward another person, a woman was the most common recipient. This aggression was most commonly treated with a lack of protest from the female targets. Thus it is clear that whether men or women direct pornography, it still promotes a view of sex where men dominate, and are aggressive, toward women.[159]

In my recent interview with Dr. Rebecca Whisnant, a philosopher from the University of Dayton who has spoken for many decades about the harms of pornography, she points to a shift she has seen in pro-porn arguments.

> "I noticed over the past couple of decades a real change in the kinds of questions that I would tend to be asked when I would teach about the issue or give slide shows or lectures. Back in the 90s, if there were critical questions, it was all about censorship and the law, arguing that this is protected free speech under the First Amendment. In the last decade the questions are different: when people are inclined to be opposed to what I am saying, they are asking 'what about feminist porn?' That is, 'aren't you aware of this burgeoning practice of creating feminist porn which isn't like what you are talking about and is liberatory?' Sometimes it was from people who seemed to know what they were talking about, in the sense that they had seen some of this material and thought it was good. Other times it was people who didn't want to be seen as prudish or opposed to all sexual representations, and who had heard that there was such a thing as feminist pornography and wanted to know what I thought of that, if there was such a thing, and would I be against it."

After hearing much talk about this niche genre that the pornography industry titles "feminist porn," Dr. Whisnant decided to study the issue in-depth. She selected a financially successful pornographer who identifies as feminist to study her work: Tristan Taormino. One of her first realizations about Taormino's work was that rather than being made as a separate enterprise from mainstream pornography, Taormino coordinates closely with the larger industry. Dr. Whisnant noted,

> "The relationship between many self-described feminist pornographers and the mainstream industry is very cozy, from what I can discern. For example, Tristan Taormino prides herself on working hand in glove with the mainstream industry, and to her credit she is very forthcoming about that relationship; it's not like she is trying to hide it. And she is forthcoming about the fact that this has involved certain kinds of compromises and things that she might not otherwise have done. The way that she got her first movie made is that she approached many mainstream pornographers to make it, to fund it, and finally she was able to get (a high profile pornographer) to do it and he was the executive producer. He is a very prominent mainstream gonzo pornographer, and she goes to him hat in hand, saying, 'I want you to make this.'"

The 'feminist' genre of pornography is one more effort by a multi-billion dollar industry to make more money by diversifying their product labels. As Dr. Whisnant noted,

> "I do think in some cases it becomes more of a niche marketing thing than anything else ... There is certainly an element in the pornography industry

that looks to make its products attractive to a broader audience by calling it 'feminist porn.' It is in the interest of the industry as a whole to have another niche market of material that labels itself feminist."

As to whether pornography can meet a commonly accepted definition of feminist, Dr. Whisnant strongly suggests that it cannot.

"No pornography that I have ever seen, that I am aware of in any way, shape or form, is consistent with my operational definition of what is feminist. To me, for some kind of sexual or erotic material to qualify as feminist, just for starters, it would have to exist outside what Andrea Dworkin defined as the nature and function of pornography, which is that it sexualizes hierarchy, objectification, submission and violence. And so basically, feminist sexual material would have to not sexualize any of those things."

I asked Dr. Whisnant how feminist pornographers supported the assertion that their work is in accordance with feminist understandings. She noted,

"What makes the difference to them, what makes material 'feminist' in their view, is 'authenticity.' That is, it's not scripted, it is not fake, it represents the real desires of the people who are performing, particularly the women. Another element that is supposed to make 'feminist porn' different is mixing up roles and representations, so that it is not always men shown being dominant and women in a submissive role. You can have women being dominant and men being submissive ... So mixing up who does what is a big element. Also there's an emphasis on more diversity of representation in general. Taormino says that she always makes sure there are performers of color in her films, for example. And supposedly, although I haven't really noticed it, there is more diversity of body type and body size and so on."

Among the strongest arguments that pornography and feminism are at odds with each other is the objectifying nature of porn. Dr. Whisnant observed,

"I think there are hard questions about what a graphic representation of sexuality could be that doesn't sexualize objectification in some sense. But what is very clear in looking at the materials and the writings of these people who fancy themselves feminist pornographers or feminist porn performers is what I've described here has nothing to do with their conception of what feminist porn is. Their conception of feminist porn is completely consistent with the sexualizing of hierarchy, objectification, submission, and violence—including, though not limited to, material in which women bear the brunt of these practices. A number of these people make a point of denying that their conception of feminism has anything to do with rejecting dominance or hierarchy or pain or violence. And if you look at the material, it is pretty clear that it doesn't, since it is full of all of those things." Thus, feminist porn is an oxymoron.

Pro-porn feminists like Taormino try to brand their pornography as "organic, fair-trade porn." When I read her book, *The Feminist*

Porn Book, I had hoped to find a clear articulation of a feminist porn perspective, informed by the systematic collection of data in some scholarly form. That is not want I discovered. I read one chapter after another written by someone apparently tied to the porn industry writing about how the kind of porn they create or support is a great thing, with no real evidence to support half-baked conclusions.

Taormino shares essays that support the narrative propagated by the pornography industry that acting in pornography is empowering to women. The editors of *The Feminist Porn Book* include professors and pornographers who seek to show how the goals of feminism and the actions in pornography are consistent. They define feminist porn as a genre that "uses sexually explicit imagery to contest and complicate the dominant representations of gender, sexuality, race, ethnicity, class, ability, age, body type, and other identity markers." (page 9). While reading through the book, I was struck by the disconnect between authors who claim that people who identify as anti-porn feminists have become hostile to scholarly work, juxtaposed against the lack of empirical research cited to support their points of view. Authors like Clarissa Smith and Fiona Attwood blame anti-porn feminists for being hostile to research, while citing nothing empirical to support their claims.[160]

Others who have read Taormino's book are equally critical of the writing and of the arguments therein. For example, Dr. Whisnant observed,

> "In *The Feminist Porn Book* that came out a couple of years ago, one of the pieces that I find chilling is by Betty Dodson. She says at one point, and this is a very common view in defenses not only of feminist porn but of porn generally, that all sexuality is imbued with dominance and power, with 'power exchange.' So the belief is that power

and dominance in sex are inevitable, and if you don't think your sex life has that in it then you are just wrong, you are in denial, you can't face those gritty truths of sexuality."

Ultimately, when a pro-porn, allegedly feminist argument is made, it comes up rather empty. As Dr. Robert Jensen noted in our recent interview,

> "The most recent book was called *The Feminist Porn Book*. It came out 3 or 4 years ago. I went through it; none of it seemed to make a compelling case, for anything ... The question I ask when people argue for feminist porn or egalitarian porn is 'why do you need pictures?' ... We live in this hyper-mediated society which increasingly says nothing is real if it is not mediated."

Lately, some feminist porn has morphed into a new money-making genre of so-called "ethical porn." In a recent post on social media, Dr. Gail Dines remarked about this particular oxymoron.

> "So called 'ethical porn' is a marketing ploy to pull so called progressives into accepting an industry that is, at its core, corrupt and misogynist. Any monetizing and commodifying of women's bodies by the sex industry is inherently abusive and can never be ethical or "fair trade." How does one "fair trade" the buying and selling of human bodies? Brilliant strategy on behalf of the industry to legitimize that which should never be legitimate in an equal and just society," (Gail Dines, Facebook, 7/30/15).

John D. Foubert, Ph.D.

Liberating and Empowering?

Part of the academic word salad referred to earlier by Dr. Jensen is the notion that acting in pornography is a liberating experience that the actresses find empowering. A member of the audience made this type of argument where Dr. Walter DeKeseredy gave a presentation on his book *Violence Against Women in Pornography.* He noted,

> "I was in England giving a presentation about pornography, and I was sharply attacked by a female graduate student who said that 'you are oppressing my sexuality, this is liberatory' and so on, so I said, 'I think you and I are talking about two different types of sexual material. I'm talking about gonzo,' and I made it very explicit. She was really, really aggressive about this, and I was like, 'Whoa! We are not going to agree about this, and that is fine, but I need to understand something. Could you explain to me what is liberating about (a particularly violent act that occurs in mainstream pornography)? And I really wanted to know how is that liberating. There was dead silence in the room. She had no answer."

One author who makes the argument that women experience pornography acting as liberating is Rich Moreland. In his book, *Pornography feminism: As powerful as she wants to be,* he makes the argument that being in porn is an expression of women's "personal sexual agency, their art, and their politics" (p. 1). With the vague term "art" inserted into an equation where violence against women is the norm; an attempt is made to sidestep the inherent violence in pornography. The word "art" does not make violence acceptable. To an extent, the word "art" is used to sanitize the violence. In addition, the word "political" implies something that anyone can have an opinion on and that nobody can question an opinion's veracity or strength. It's just political, so how can you question it? However, the language of politics does not match the reality of pornography.[161] As this very book describes repeatedly, the harms of pornography are clear.

It's About The Money

Many academics that are pro-porn seem to misunderstand or ignore the intent and effect of the pornography industry; in particular, they misunderstand the economics of pornography. Recently, Dr. Gail Dines attended a conference in London put on by pro-pornography academic groups. In my interview with her, she reflected,

> "They are all academics, they are all pro-porn, they have no understanding of a political economy. They had an opening keynote session speaker say there is no such thing as a porn business. Why? Because there is too much porn. My response to that is can you imagine being at a car conference and they say there is no such thing as a car industry because there are too many cars on the road? It is crazy. The fact that they [pornography businesses] have so many products, the fact that they have trade shows, the fact they have business websites, all show that this is what we call a 'maturing business.' So one of the things I'm doing is showing people how to follow the money as a way to show the bankruptcy of the pro-porn analysis." Dines continues, "The pro-porn people brand pornography as a fun, hip, edgy kind of thing. When you follow the money what you see is that it is a business, it is nothing about sexual fantasy, it is nothing about creativity, it is about maximizing the dollar. So if you follow the money, you wipe out the idiocy of the pro-porn movement that doesn't understand how it is a business."

One glaring omission from the arguments made by pro-porn academics is evidence. Little is offered beyond thought essays and personal anecdotes. The few empirical studies that are cited by these academics typically run counter to the mountain of available research in the area. This observation is made by Dr. Dines about pro-porn activists.

> "They do not use empirical evidence, even the academics! They have no evidence to back up their claims. What they do have is an occasional junk science study ... They have hooked on to maybe two or three studies that are out there, which when you go over them with a fine tooth comb, methodologically they are deeply flawed. Now, all studies obviously have methodological flaws. You can't ever conduct social science research with a perfect study. But you can look at methodological triangulation – what are all the methods that we are using and what is the picture that is showing."

In contrast to the perspective of pro-porn academics, Dr. Dines goes on to note the orientation of people who speak out against pornography.

> "So the interesting thing is that the anti-porn people are the ones in the academy who are rooted in academic research. The other side just comes out with some discursive analysis of what goes on and says it is empowering to women. They never mention, what does empowering mean? How many women have you interviewed? What are you using to measure empowerment? It is all very well for you to say it is empowering, but what do you mean? There is no empirical evidence of that. It is conjecture; ideological statements that have no basis in any research."

A Pro-Porn Academic Journal?

In one more attempt to insert a pro-pornography stance into mainstream culture, a group of academics, many with ties to the pornography industry, started a new academic journal in 2014, published by Routledge, a division of Taylor & Francis. It is unabashedly pro-porn, thus moving away from the core purpose of academic journals, to publish scholarly work judged on the strength of its methods rather than the direction of its conclusions. In introducing this new journal, the editors (and by extension, Routledge) essentially scoff at more than 50 studies demonstrating the link between pornography and sexual violence, arguing that a connection between the two is merely "putative" or assumed and undemonstrated. Even if all 50 studies used the lowest possible standard of evidence (a 5% likelihood that results could be due to chance), the odds that all 50 studies finding the same thing are simply due to chance and don't reflect a systematic problem is 1 in 88,817,841,970,012,523,233,890,533,447,265,625. That is one in eighty-eight dectrillion, eight-hundred-seventeen nonillion, eight-hundred-forty-one octillion, nine-hundred seventy septillion, twelve sextillion, five-hundred-twenty-three pentrillion, two-hundred-thirty-three quadrillion, eight-hundred-ninety trillion, five-hundred-thirty-three billion, four-hundred-forty-seven million, two-hundred-sixty-five thousand, six-hundred and twenty-five. One way to think about this is if you had to randomly select a specific penny from a mountain of pennies representing the amount of the national debt of the United States, you would have much better odds of randomly selecting the right penny than the odds that all 50 of these studies are wrong. Another way to say it is that the editors of *Porn Studies* would rather take a chance that they can randomly extract the right penny from this mountain than admit that pornography leads to violence against women. Which odds will you go with?[162]

John D. Foubert, Ph.D.

By creating a journal that denies the effects of pornography on sexual violence, the editors are openly supporting the violence against women found in today's pornography, which, in turn, is then re-enacted by men toward women all over the world. Journal editors also deny that there is increasing violence in pornography, ignoring a mountain of published evidence to the contrary. Rather than inviting scholarship that is based in rigorous scientific methods, the editors simply ask that authors write articles where the methods are 'clear.' With that logic, any manuscript could be clearly flawed as long as they are clear about how they are flawed. If the articles published by that journal are any indication thus far, the journal is unlikely to print anything that can remotely be called scholarly.

A Concluding Thought

Ultimately, most arguments made by pro-porn academics and other activists are either logically inconsistent, void of supporting evidence, ploys to make more money by supporting violence against women, or some combination thereof. It certainly seems counterintuitive that people would claim a feminist label while actively working to undermine the liberation of women by objectifying them.

Chapter 10

Current Trends in Pornography: New Technologies, "Ethical Porn," and Extreme Violence

The pornography industry has come a long way since the advent of Playboy Magazine. Shortly before *How Pornography Harms* went to press, Playboy had just decided to stop printing nude photos; it seems that the availability of Internet pornography gave them too much competition. And to today's digital generation, magazines are passé.[163] Most of the pornography accessed today isn't in a magazine or in a movie one watches in a theater or at home. Most pornography is accessed through websites, and viewed on portable computers or phones of some sort or another. In 2010, there were over 4 million pornography websites on the Internet, with 10,000 being added every week.[164]

Over time, the pornography industry has adapted new technologies in order to make higher profits from their growing consumer base. The overarching theme of change has been the making of more interactive and more violent pornography. In the 12 years between 1986 and 1998, explicit media showed a significant increase in "unaffectionate sex," which is characterized by sexual acts devoid of "warmth, care, or love" [165] (Peter & Valkenburg, 2010, p. 359).

In their summary of the research on pornography done in this time span, Peter and Valkenburg found that pornography was increasingly defined by themes of male dominance in which a male used a female as a sole means of his own satisfaction without regard to her sexual desires or gratification. The authors summarized that during that span of time, the portrayal of unaffectionate sexual encounters increased in frequency from 54% to 94% of pornographic scenes. The authors concluded that the pornography from previous decades that had once showed a consensual sexual experience between partners has evolved into a woman-hating act of male domination and self-satisfaction.[166] This trend has continued throughout the 21st century.[167] As a result, more and more people believe that their viewing of extreme pornography is normal.[168] In this chapter, I will point out some of the trends in pornography that are occurring into the latter half of the 2010's.

Few would question that technology is changing rapidly, and along with it, the delivery systems for pornography. Younger people typically embrace new technology in each successive generation. As of 2014, 95% of 12 to 17 year olds in the United States had Internet access; 74% had access through a mobile device.[169] In my interview with Greg, a Christian man who has fought a pornography addiction for a decade, he noted, "Smart phones changed the game. A lot of times I have my phone locked where I don't have the Internet, I don't have my phone apps. I just use it as an iPod and a text message machine. I need to do that again. This bout in the spring where I had so much success I had all my apps blocked. It helps to have no means of accessing pornography so that would help. Such a useful device, a phone, can also be so destructive."

New(er) Terms and Technologies

Now that smart phones are ubiquitous, they are being used to spread pornography. Simultaneously, the pornography industry has pushed the development of new technologies and new terms by which to make money from consumers through the exploitation of (mostly) women. An increasingly common practice, especially by high school and college students, is sexting. Depending upon the content of the image, in some cases a sext message can easily fall into the category of pornography, even child pornography. In some cases, prosecutors have agreed.[170]

<u>Sexting</u>

Concurrent with the societal trend toward more people having smart phones with cameras, and more people at younger ages using them, a rise in sharing photographs has occurred. Some of these photographs capture either the owner of the phone, or someone who happens to be in the presence of the owner, naked. As the practice of sharing naked photographs through smart phones became more popular, the term "sexting" emerged to describe the practice. While some have broad definitions of sexting that include sexually explicit written messages, I will limit my review to those messages that contain images.

So what exactly is being sent through sext messages? A recent study analyzed their content. About one-in-five sext messages were pictures of children 15 years old or younger. Of those pictures, almost all were taken with a webcam and almost all were of girls.[171] Why do teens sext? The most common reasons are to invite sexual activity, to get a partner or potential partner's attention, to flirt, because their dating partner pressured them into it, and to express themselves.[172] [173]

Several recent studies have sought to determine how frequently high school and college students engage in sexting. Studies about high school student sexting tend to be done on college students, asking them about their behavior in high school. For example, a study of college students who were asked if they sexted when they were under 18 found that 28% sent sexts to someone else that contained pictures (over half had sent explicit messages that had only words). Teens who had sexted were largely unaware that when they sent sexual pictures of underage people (themselves or someone else) that it might have met the definition of child pornography. Interestingly, those who knew that the practice was illegal were less likely to sext. Furthermore, most teens that had sexted and did not realize at the time it could be illegal, said they would not have sexted if they knew it could be illegal.[174] Thus, it seems wise to educate teens that sexting is often illegal and should be avoided. Doing so shows promise in curbing the behavior.

Among teens who sexted, the average age when they first did so was 16. In addition to the 28% who sent photographic sext messages, over a quarter of teens had forwarded or shared a sext message with a friend. Only 2% shared sext messages with parents or teachers. Thus, it is unlikely that parents know whether their offspring have sexted. Interestingly, twice as many girls had sexted than boys, primarily in the context of a romantic relationship or in an attempt to attract the attention of a prospective partner. Over seven-in-ten teenagers knew another teen that experienced negative consequences as a result of a sexting message. The most common consequence was humiliation.[175]

One of the participants I interviewed for this book talked about his experience sexting with friends in high school. Tommy is a young-looking, lanky, attractive Caucasian male college student. He noted

> "Like, in high school, girls would take pictures of themselves, send it to guys, and guys would send it around. All the pictures got collected and they all got released massively, so they were like, 'we're going to start getting all these girls.'"

As the naked pictures of girls in his high school spread, word reached the administration of his high school. Rather than punishing those who spread the pictures, the administration focused on the girls in the images. Tommy continued,

> "They all got caught, so they called every girl in the school that was in the pictures and called them into the office. I think they just got detention, some of them could get in legal trouble for it for child pornography depending upon how old they are but most of them just got detention and stuff like that … The boys didn't get in trouble. They kinda covered it up. It kinda happened, I mean, this was a huge scandal with like 20 or 30 girls and it kinda just, once it happened, once the principal kinda found out, the kids kinda all deleted the pictures and deleted that they ever sent them, they were definitely, like, you can't catch me."

I asked Tommy why so many girls sent naked pictures of themselves to boys, and why the boys spread them around. He shared,

> "I think kids are much more likely to be aroused and be finding things more attractive with people they know than with people they don't know. So with all those girls pictures of high school girls that they knew, it was much more exciting for them instead of just random girls on the Internet, but since they knew those people, it was a lot different. Because you see those people, you see them in school and you see them and you go 'Ah, I've seen you' and it is just totally different than someone online that you'll never see."

Research is now beginning to be published about the characteristics of teenagers who sext. For example, one study found that among junior and senior high school students, especially boys, sexters are more likely than their peers to engage in intimate contact with a peer when one or both of them is already in a committed relationship.[176] Sexting teens are also more likely to watch sexually themed reality television.[177] In addition, teens that sext are more likely to engage in sexual risk taking. In particular, sexters are seven times more likely to be sexually active and about twice as likely to have unprotected sex than their peers who do not sext. In addition, girls who sent nude pictures of themselves were more likely to use alcohol or drugs prior to engaging in sexual relations.[178] [179] Thus, if a parent or pastor becomes aware that a teen is sexting, it makes sense to inquire about other related behaviors that could be a spiritual and physical threat to the person sexting.

Once students are in college, many more have participated in sexting. When college students have been asked about their sexting behavior, from their early teen years through their current age in college, a clear majority, 61%, report having sexted at some point in their lives. When researchers dug deeper into the experience of students who sexted versus those who had not, they found that sexters are 4.5 times more likely to have had unprotected sex, four times more likely to view pornography, and about 2.5 times more likely to chat online with people they don't know. These high-risk behaviors are obvious cause for concern; though of course this doesn't mean that every student who sexts also acts out sexually in other ways.[180]

Portable, Interactive Devices

An article by a porn industry trade group noted the dramatic rise in the use of tablet computers for accessing pornography. The tablet computer has become a device of choice because of its portability and larger sized screens than mobile phones. In 2012, an industry trade group predicted that the number of people who pay to use different mobile porn sites would triple in just 3 years, along with a tripling of pornography optimized for tablets. One concern the industry noted is that business growth on tablets may not grow as quickly as the industry would like, given that multiple people typically share these devices and porn users tend not to want others who share their devices to see what pornography they view.[181]

Still, the pornography industry continues to adapt and change to their market. More recent efforts are designed to make pornography more interactive. An increasingly common practice is to have pornography websites that permit interaction with live performers, where consumers can request and pay for specific acts from a performer on a webcam. In my recent interview with Dr. Gail Dines, she shared, "The next generation of porn is syncing your body and the film."

As of 2016, pornography producers had identified this sort of syncing body and film with virtual reality as the next big way to make money in porn. For those who know about how the porn industry works, this will come as no surprise. A prominent porn industry producer[182] brags that bringing virtual reality to porn is a game changer as big as the creation of the Internet. It is also described as a way to keep the money in the hands of large pornography businesses and out of the hands of people who operate small-scale porn operations. Large companies that can afford the high cost of production are the only ones who can integrate new virtual reality technology into pornographic media. The big guys see this as a way to consolidate their power, influence, and profits in the industry. Making virtual reality porn will require proprietary technology, thus the large pornography producers who will own that technology will make money from others who wish to use it as well. The kinds of experiences the new porn offers include a hologram type experience, where the user can move around a virtual room where a movie has been filmed, and look at what he wishes to see.

Small time porn makers will not be able to compete in the virtual reality marketplace because holographic content costs $50,000 per minute to make. This amount is an easy investment for a big company in an industry that makes over 10 billion dollars a year just in the United States, but next to impossible for a couple with a webcam at home.[183]

"Ethical Porn"

Over time, the pornography industry has come up with multiple terms in an attempt to capture more consumers who may have some aversion to the term "pornography" itself. These terms include "erotica," "feminist porn," and, more recently, "ethical porn." Regarding allegedly ethical porn, Dr. Dines notes

> "Ethical porn is the new argument. It is ridiculous. It's very interesting, ethical porn is how they are now branding a slice of the porn industry; it is basically a marketing tool. It is basically porn using women of different shapes and sizes, they say they talk to the women about the kinds of things that women want to do, they don't go beyond their comfort zones. We don't know that is the case because you've only got their word. My argument is look, when you look at porn production, you have to ask how a woman ended up there. And by chance, I'm sure she didn't end up there because she had a slew of life opportunities ahead of her. First of all, you are working on the backs of an oppressed group, they are economically oppressed, this is one of the few ways that they can earn money. And secondly, what

does it mean 'ethical porn?' So supposing I'm 18 and my boyfriend has told me that I'm really hot and I've been having sex for awhile for free, which is what normally happens, and my boyfriend says it is a good idea if I start charging for it. So, suppose I'm 18 and I'm living in Arkansas and I see ahead of myself minimum wage in Wal-Mart. When you are 18, you are a kid. We know that the full adult brain hasn't developed until you are 24. So I decide at 18 this looks good, so I go into it. I get into the porn industry, my images are forever captured, and by age 23, I realize I've made a terrible mistake. How am I ever going to get those images back? You are going to lose control of your image. In the age of the Internet, you can never ever get those images back. So how do we expect that 18 year old girls will come to a decision at that age and think it is ethical because they have thought it through? Real ethical porn would be saying to them, 'Look, you are 18 or 19 now, this might look like a good idea. Let's say in 5 years you've left the porn industry and you look for a job. Your image is everywhere; they can find it in two minutes. You go get a job, and if you do, you'll be fired when they find it. And you might live on and marry and have children, and your children are going to see that you did porn. It is going to follow you the rest of your life. So when you sign here on the dotted line, you are signing that you have lost control of the most intimate parts of your life. Are you ready for that?' And I'd guess the answer in most cases is no. And the other question here is what does it mean for people who you do not know, having the rights to be voyeurs to the most intimate part of your life? Do we have that right?

My answer would be no. So I don't see how you can have anything ethical that invites people into a part of your life that they have no right to be in."

Upping the Ante on Violence and Abuse

Henry, a young Hispanic college student I interviewed for this book, mentioned the rising tide of violence and degradation in pornography videos. He reported his experience seeing a video where two women were horribly degraded. "So basically two girls started out as some sort of lesbian kind of porno but then they just started [defecating and vomiting]. That is one thing that is going to stick in my memory. It was in 7ᵗʰ grade; people were talking about it of course, then like any strange thing on the Internet, it has to be discussed and of course, my curiosity led me to it. Obviously I was warned that it was very vile and your eyes will burn sort of thing, but my curiosity got the best of me. I managed to watch it as much as I can but at some point I said I don't want to watch this anymore, I don't know why anyone would make this …"

Regarding more violent pornography, Tommy noted,

> "I've seen like weird stuff like fisting and stuff like that, I don't look for that, I look for just standard stuff. [Fisting] looks painful, it doesn't seem attractive. I don't think that stuff like anal or fisting is that attractive."

Similarly, Greg recounted violence against women he saw in pornography when he was in junior high school,

> "A long time ago, when I was a junior in high school, I think the worst thing I've ever seen was (sigh), sex toys (being used on a woman) that are

like too big, you know? Obviously like her body has been manipulated somehow to make that possible. It is portrayed as chauvinistic 'woman I'm going to show you' thing. At the time, it was probably arousing honestly but it was also horrifying and so I steered clear of that."

This kind of extreme violence seems to have increased greatly during the last decade or two. As Dr. Robert Jensen recounts,

"I think it is safe to say that especially with the Internet there is a dramatic increase in men's habitual use of pornography. I hear all the time from people who say I would love to stop using this, I just can't stop. That was always present, but the Internet has ratcheted up the intensity of porn and the availability of porn so I think the problem is even more dramatic than 20 years ago."

Messi is a young Hispanic college male, whose short fuzzy beard hides a bit of his engaging smile. He talked about the violence he sees against women in today's pornography,

"The girls in the pornography I have seen have been in pain. Some of the positions look painful. The position looks like they might be in pain but they don't show it on their face. Ones where they are super spread out to where it shouldn't be a position, where you have that extra flexibility."

Revenge Porn

State and federal laws are often slow to keep up with the rapidly changing nature of practices that a reasonable person would think should be illegal. For example, laws have been slow to keep up with the phenomenon of revenge porn. Revenge porn is defined as

> "pornography in which at least one of the subjects was unaware that sexual acts were being fixed in a tangible medium of expression or was unaware of or opposed to the work's distribution, usually over the Internet." (p. 44).

> What makes revenge porn so insidious is that the images, once uploaded to the Internet, can never be reliably removed. Thus, others seeing those pictures in perpetuity can continually victimize an individual.[184]

A typical example, reported by legal scholars, is the case of a man who takes naked pictures of his girlfriend with her consent, as long as he agrees not to show others. After they break up, he shares the photos on a special site created for the purpose of uploading revenge porn pictures. He does so along with her name and contact information. Because she consented to have the photos taken, his posting them without her permission is currently not illegal.[185] It is estimated that there are now thousands of websites where people can upload naked/pornographic pictures of a former partner for everyone in the world to see. On these sites, most of the people who upload images are male; most pictures are of women.[186]

Some revenge porn images and videos are made by men with the consent of the women they were intimately involved with, but then distributed online without their consent after their relationship has ended.[187] Though prosecutions and other legal action against people who post revenge porn are rare, legal scholars are beginning to suggest that the practice of posting naked photos of someone without their permission may be able to be declared obscene, and thus illegal.[188]

Rape Porn

As you know from reading this book, violence in pornography is now mainstream. One kind of extreme violence in pornography is acting out a rape. Depicting rape in pornography used to be rather rare; it is now a practice with increasing frequency and acceptance among pornography users. One reason why the existence of rape pornography is so disturbing is that men who watch rape pornography are more likely to fantasize about raping a woman, and are more likely to believe that women secretly wish to be raped and/or enjoy experiencing rape.[189] Not surprisingly, most rape porn includes a male perpetrator and a female victim. On some websites that serve as a repository for types of porn, consumers are allowed to make comments on the videos so that others can consider a review before viewing a particular movie or clip. One illustrative quote from a man who viewed a rape porn film noted that the one improvement that could be made was if it were a real rape rather than one that was simply acted out.[190]

In two studies I conducted with colleagues, including Dr. Matt Brosi and Dr. Sean Bannon, we researched the impact of violent pornography on fraternity men and sorority women. We found that exposure to rape pornography and sadomasochistic pornography was higher than expected. During just one year, 19% of fraternity men and 27% of sorority women had viewed rape pornography. In addition, 27% of fraternity men and 21% of sorority women had viewed sadomasochistic pornography. The impact of this exposure was harmful on many fronts. For example, men who viewed violent pornography during the last year were more likely to commit rape and were less likely to intervene to help someone who might experience rape. Similarly, sorority women who viewed violent pornography during the last year were less likely to help a female friend who might experience sexual violence and had stronger beliefs supporting rape.[191] [192] These results undermine the supposition that pornography use is just a personal issue. It is not. When people view violent pornography, they become more dangerous to be around. This is the case both with the increased likelihood that they will act out what they have seen in pornography and the decreased likelihood they will step in to help a friend who might experience sexual assault.

A Concluding Thought

As the pornography industry continues to grow, they have been highly successful in making money from exploiting people's bodies. They facilitate as much interaction with their product as possible and find more ways to insert violence into sexual situations, even to the point of rape. Given how common violence is in pornography, if you or someone you know is watching pornography for any length of time, odds are, what is being watched includes violence, sometimes extreme violence. Given the penchant of the porn industry to make pornography more violent, and more realistic, a great hope is that people in jury pools (like you) will be more open to declaring pornography obscene, thus illegal, sending pornographers where they can do the least damage – in prison.

Chapter 11

How Porn is Changing the Way People are Having Sex

There are numerous behaviors that occur during sexual encounters; some God honoring, some not. While there is some degree of variability in how people behave sexually, for the most part, there are a limited number of activities that one can engage in given human design and limitations. Many of the participants I interviewed for this book do not hold a Biblical worldview, and even when some do, many still act outside the bounds of God's design for sex between husband and wife. Some of their experiences, as influenced by pornography, are described in this chapter not to endorse the behavior, but to further describe the total depravity encouraged by pornography.

Sexual Scripts

If you think about where you learned the most about sex, you likely learned about it from peers, maybe parents, or more likely from some form of media – print, still pictures, or moving pictures. Those tend to be the primary sources of information people use to figure out what sex is[193]. When peers or the media describe sex, it usually includes more than just "insert tab A into slot B." The specifics you are told, or shown, likely include some series of events, that lead to more events, leading to highly stimulating events, and then after a time, the scenario ends. A description of a series of events is a kind of script – something in your mind that is an expectation for how a series of events play out. When these expectations play out in a sexual encounter, our expectations form a sexual script.[194]

The concept of a sexual script is something that scholars who study the impact of media on behavior have studied for a long time. The research of several scholars demonstrates that the expectations we have for an event – such as sexual intercourse – are set with an anticipated series of behaviors that we have laid out in our brain.[195] [196] We typically carry this script forward into our behavior and act it out. When studying pornography, many scholars use the term "script" to mean the unwritten messages conveyed in a form of media that are encoded in the brain as a way behavior is expected to occur in real life.

One of the ways that these scripts can hurt us, and other people, is when the set of behaviors we expect, or request from others, harms one or more people in an encounter. This is where pornography comes in. When people view today's mainstream pornography, especially repeatedly and over time, it encodes a script in their brain that includes behavior that ranges from violent to extremely violent.[197] When these scripts are carried out, they can harm other participants in a sexual encounter. The sexual scripts we learn from pornography are rewriting the way people are engaging in sexual intercourse. Moreover, a 2015 nationwide study found that the impact of pornography is increasing.[198] This increased impact is correlated with increased use.

Increasing Use Over Time

As more people are digital natives each year, and as the generation that has grown up with unrestricted access to pornography enters adulthood, the portion of the total population that has viewed pornography has increased. In the 1970s, 45% of men viewed x rated movies. The next national study, in the 1990s, found that 61% were viewing x rated movies, just before the Internet boom.[199] After the Internet made pornography readily available in the first decade of the 21st Century, research showed that 86% of men were viewing pornography.[200] [201]

As for young adult women, 28% had viewed an x rated movie in the 1970s.[202] Post-Internet, this increased to 36%. Clearly, the use of pornography is increasing. For children born in the 1980s and later, they are the first to have Internet access in their teens. The main reason for the increase in pornography use in recent decades is the advent of Internet pornography.

Theories

This increased use of pornography, nearly universal for young men, imbeds a set of sexual scripts into their psyche, which then plays out in their behavior.[203] There are several theories that apply the concept of a script to sexual behavior. They have many similarities; with some nuances that together help us better understand the phenomenon in question.

Social Cognitive Theory

One theory is social learning theory, also called social cognitive theory, by Dr. Albert Bandura.[204] Psychologists have long understood that much of our behavior is impacted by what we see others do. Social psychologist Albert Bandura showed that people tend to behave in ways they see others behave, particularly when the behavior they observe leads to positive outcomes. A contemporary psychologist, Dr. Ana Bridges, observes that Bandura's theory is highly applicable to how pornography affects the viewer. She notes that when we view the behavior of others, it is more likely that we will imitate that behavior if we believe the actor is like us. Pornography, she notes, teaches us how to be sexual with other people, how we achieve pleasure ourselves, and potentially, how to give pleasure to others.[205] Given the violence in pornography and the obvious spiritual depravity it represents, the lessons it teaches are devastatingly harmful.

Cognitive Script Theory

A closely related theory to social cognitive theory is cognitive script theory. Dr. Chyng Sun and her colleagues, whose research we have seen throughout this book, often utilize this theory. Using cognitive script theory, this research team explains that the behavioral patterns (scripts) we see in the media create a model for us to make decisions when we find ourselves in situations similar to the media we have ingested. The more frequently an individual sees the same script play itself out, the more they remember them and the more likely they are to act on those scripts. They note that the script that plays out on most mainstream pornography is one where men inflict violence and degrading acts toward women. They found that, the more pornography a man watches, the more he also watches porn on a mobile device *during* a sexual encounter. Increased amounts of time spent watching pornography are also associated with asking his partner to do things he saw in porn, having to think about what he saw in porn to remain aroused, and being concerned with how he performs sexually. Rather than being an enhancement to a sexual encounter, this research team found that the more men use porn, the less they enjoy sex and the worse they feel about how their body looks.[206]

3AM Theory

Another theory that helps us understand sexual scripts is the 3AM theory postulated by Dr. Paul Wright. Dr. Wright has developed a model intended to address why the same media content affects different people in different ways. In my recent interview with Dr. Wright, he explained,

> "The model is broken down into three component parts: the acquisition of sexual scripts, the activation of sexual scripts, and the application of sexual scripts. Acquisition refers to the learning of a novel sexual script, activation refers to the priming of an already acquired sexual script, and application refers to the use of a sexual script to inform a perception, judgment, or behavior. At each step of the process there are variables that are hypothesized to increase or decrease the likelihood of each effect, such as particulars of the sexual portrayal, states and traits of the audience, and situational factors surrounding the perceptual, judgmental, or behavioral environment."

Essentially, Dr. Wright's theory is that people learn ways of engaging in sexual behavior through a variety of means, particularly the media. These learned ways of behaving can be triggered by different things in a person's environment. People can then choose to act on those triggered learned ways of behaving, or can decide not to behave according to the particular learned behavior.

Unrealistic Expectations

The average young adult has sexual intercourse two to four years after they see pornography for the first time. Thus, pornography use most often precedes intercourse. This use of pornography is shown by research to set people up for unrealistic expectations for their sexual encounters – whether those encounters are between husband and wife or not.[207]

One research participant I interviewed who spoke of these unrealistic expectations is Ella. Ella is an African American woman, a mother, in her 20s. She noted,

> "I think pornography for both women and men makes both of us feel that we have to perform a certain way, that we have to try out these new positions, have this stamina, have three orgasms, or have a guy who is pretty big down there. There may be a guy who is watching it who may not fit what, like, that guy on the screen is like; he may feel weird about himself, he may try to overcompensate for that in the bedroom because he might think that a woman might want that from him - the same for women. We may think that we are not making certain facial features like the girls on the porn videos so that if I do that my significant other won't like me anymore or be more intimate with me."

Jack also described some insecurity. After seeing a lot of pornography before he first had intercourse, he noted that he felt pressure "to be able to do the actions he [the actor in pornography] did, I needed to have the plumbing he had, everything. The whole shebang." Another man, Bob, a Native American college student in his 20s remarked, "on those videos the men have really big ones so when I'm having sex I wonder if she is, like, pleasured enough. I don't know." Bob continued in our interview to reflect on whether his penis was large enough to satisfy his girlfriend, with whom he is sexually active.

John, another man I interviewed, is about 30 years old; he had many expectations of how sex is supposed to play out, based on the pornography he has viewed. If viewed through Dr. Wright's model, John acquired and activated scripts from pornography, but when he tried to apply them, they didn't go very well. John recalled,

> "When I first had sex, I thought I was using all my encounters from porn, trying to do different positions, trying to make things up, it was all based on the porn I had seen. I told the girl [during sex], 'This is boring,' and she got mad and left. Looking back on it today, that 100% had to do with my view of what porn was and how that translated into sex. I was 18. I don't know what I was trying to do, but I was basing it all on the porn I had watched from a young age." I asked John what he expected and then did not experience based on pornography. He replied, "based on how the girl is supposed to react, she is supposed to be making noises, begging for more, everything you see in a porno I was trying to recreate in the sexual experience I was with. It didn't go well at all. I was trying to be too similar to that and wasn't being myself. I was trying to be too creative I guess and not letting things go how they go. Not making that connection one-on-one rather than trying to do the physical things you see in a porno. We were having sex to have sex, not to build a connection."

Tommy is a young college student whose pornography use set his expectations for sex. He recalled,

> "Before I had sex with my girlfriend, it [pornography] kinda, like, taught me what to do. It makes it easier,

it makes it more interesting. I know what a girl likes, kinda, you can tell, whether she really likes that or not as much. It helps to, like, learn what they expect, what you think they will like – it helps to start there so you have something to go off of."

Tommy also spoke about how seeing pornography made him less satisfied with his sexual partner, consistent with the research mentioned earlier by Drs. Sun, Bridges, Johnson, and Ezzell. He noted,

"In movies and pornography, they make it very, very attractive, very naked so that you are really turned on by it and sometimes when I am with my girlfriend, it is just not as sexual, and maybe she thinks it is, but I'm just not as turned on as she is in the moment. It's kinda like I'm seeking more from her, like I've seen in the videos, like I want to see more of that, I want to see this, I want to hear you say different things and it's just not as, as arousing."

Finally, Jennifer, a Native American Christian woman who is a wife and a mother, noted how her husband's pornography use affects her.

"I guess the way that he viewed it makes me self-conscious; if he pictures me that way or if he wishes I look that way, the way the girls do in porn. I think it makes me feel pretty self-conscious about myself and always wanting to change my body image with him because, after two kids, I look different."

Which comes first? Watching porn or having certain attitudes about sex?

Dr. Wright, whose theory we just discussed, has studied many issues including the chicken and egg question of, as he put it,

> "whether pornography affects attitudes and behaviors or whether people with particular attitudes and behavioral patterns selectively expose themselves to pornography. We pretty consistently find that prior pornography consumption predicts the later attitude or behavior under study." He also noted, "the converse doesn't necessarily seem to be true. For example, in one of my first longitudinal studies I predicted that people already engaging in casual sex would also be more likely to subsequently consume porn and people who were consuming porn would more likely in the future to engage in casual sex."

He found half of this to be true. If people watched pornography early in his study, they were more likely to have casual sex later in the study, especially people who were unhappy with their lives. In fact, people who were classified as being unhappy with their lives were seven times more likely to have casual sex if they used pornography, compared to unhappy people who did not use pornography.[208] He also found that if people had casual sex earlier in the study, it had nothing to do with whether they were watching pornography later in the study. Thus, the effect of pornography seems one way. Pornography leads to casual sexual behaviors, not the other way around.

One reason why pornography seemed to affect unhappy people more than others is that people tend to apply what they learn from the media if they are more impulsive and have less ability than most to think through the consequences of their actions. So, when people are apathetic about the long term negative effects of their behavior and more interested in changing how they feel in the short term, they are more likely to apply what they learn in pornography to their sex lives.[209]

Porn and sexual violence

By the year 2000, there were 49 experimental studies showing that the use of pornography leads to either worsening attitudes toward sexual violence or an increase in violent behavior. Drs. Neil Malamuth, Tamara Addison and Mary Koss conducted a comprehensive review of studies published up until that point about pornography and sexual assault. Specifically, they found that 16 studies, involving over 2,000 people, demonstrated that after people view pornography, they are more likely to believe that sexual violence is acceptable. An additional 33 laboratory studies involving over 2,000 people revealed that pornography caused an increase in aggressive behavior. The term "caused" can be used in this context given that an experimental research design was used. These 33 studies established that exposure to both nonviolent and violent pornography causes both aggressive attitudes and behavior, with violent pornography having a stronger effect. The researchers also found that men who are at high risk for committing sexual violence also tend to like to view violent pornography more than low risk men. This pornography viewing by high-risk men seemed to be more influential on them, encouraging them to commit sexual violence.[210] Since the year 2000, the weight of the scientific evidence continues to strongly support the conclusion that viewing pornography and committing acts of sexual aggression are inextricably intertwined. In more recent studies of the sexual behaviors of the general public, this link bears out.[211] It is important to acknowledge that these and other studies do not say that every person who watches pornography will commit sexual violence. There is not a one-to-one relationship between pornography use and rape. However, the more violent the pornography, the more often it is used, and the more a man has characteristics that put him at increased risk for committing violence, the more likely he is to be sexually violent.

Part of the reason for the association between pornography and sexual violence, is that pornography encourages men to look at potential sexual partners as objects, and not as people. As Dr. Wright observed in our recent interview, "One element of the accumulated literature that is interesting to me is the consistency of certain correlations. For example, between pornography consumption and more impersonal sexual attitudes, objectified cognitions about women, and attitudes supportive of violence against women. This speaks to the consistency of scripts related to these areas in popular pornography. If popular pornography was highly diverse in its presentation of sex, results from survey studies, for example, would be far more idiosyncratic and wide-ranging on these outcomes."

Watching and Doing

The script of sexual behavior that plays out in pornography tends to include actions that can seem novel to the viewer, placed in a form of media designed to entice. Current and ongoing research findings show that people are increasingly taking the images they see in pornography and attempting to act them out in real life. For example, Dr. Chyng Sun's research team, including Dr. Ana Bridges, is currently carrying out a series of studies in this area. According to Dr. Bridges,

> "for aggressor behaviors … … we found that men were more likely to report engaging in those behaviors than women; that is consistent with the script. We also found that the more pornography use by both men and women, the more likely they

were to engage in aggressive behaviors in sex with a partner. Both men and women, when they used porn, were more likely to engage in aggressive behaviors. It wasn't like men were at an elevated risk, which is what we thought, because typically the aggressors in porn are men, so we thought, 'if you are looking at it and you are identifying with the male character, you are more likely to do that.' But if you are not identifying with the male character, say you are a woman, maybe you are not more likely to take that because that is something guys do. We didn't find evidence of that. More porn, more aggressor behaviors in sex for both men and women, although men were more likely to do that."

Porn specific behaviors in sex

There are many acts which scholars refer to as "porn specific behaviors," meaning actions that are common in pornography but not as common in real life. One of the people who conducts this research is Dr. Paul Wright. He and his research team researched porn specific behaviors,

"behaviors that few people are socialized to engage in but are common in pornography. We reasoned that given the general perception of these behaviors as antisocial, or at least non-normative, men may need an additional disinhibiting influence to attempt these behaviors. Based on prior research on the effect of alcohol on men's sexually aggressive behavior, we looked at whether the combination of heavy pornography consumption and alcohol consumption most strongly predicted men's engagement in these behaviors. Men who had enacted the largest number of these behaviors were both those who were heavy consumers of pornography and who also regularly consumed alcohol before and during sex. So this provides an illustration that acquisition and activation do not necessarily translate to application."[212]

Drs. Bridges, Sun, Ezzell, and Johnson conducted a similar study, which Dr. Bridges told me about in a recent interview. The results she shared are preliminary, and should appear in a more complete form in an article soon. They analyzed "degrading or uncommon behaviors." They found that men are more likely to do these things to women, and that men's pornography use significantly increased the chance that men would do these things to women. They also found that the more men watched pornography, the more they wanted to do these things to women (regardless of whether they had); men who used porn more frequently also wanted their female partner to be more aggressive with them during sex.

Porn affects women's acceptance of violent sex

Dr. Bridges, along with Drs. Sun, Ezzell, and Johnson, did a follow-up study for their paper on how pornography affects men, by studying the impact on women. In my interview with Dr. Bridges, she noted that she and her research team explored women's pornography use and how that impacted their sexual encounters. Women were asked whether they experienced a number of violent behaviors targeted toward them. They found that women were more often the targets of these behaviors than men. In addition, if women used pornography, they were more likely to have been a target of these violent behaviors.

Not only were women who use pornography more likely to be a target of these behaviors, they also were more likely to be aggressors.

Dr. Bridges noted, "Pornography use is elevating aggression in sex for both men and women." She also noted that men are more likely to be the aggressor and women the target.

Watching Porn While Engaging in Sex

Dr. Bridges and her associates also found that men who use pornography are more likely to watch pornography with their partner during a sexual encounter. The more a man used pornography, the more he had to conjure up images of porn while he was having sex, to maintain his arousal. Furthermore, male porn users were more likely "to ask a partner to try something they saw in porn, and to role play a porn scene with a sexual partner. 36% asked a partner to try something they saw in pornography."

Makynlee, an African American woman about 30 years old, noted that her husband uses pornography frequently, and sometimes while they are having sex.

> "Just in the act of having sex or randomly turning it on, looking over and my husband is watching it on his phone, just different things. *While* having sex, he's watching it on his phone. Sometimes over the weekend we are just watching TV and he'll just be watching porn. We are in an open communication relationship. It doesn't bother either one of us to watch it. Better watch it than do it with someone else (she then laughed nervously). We've been together for almost 10 years, its kinda like, meh. Seen it, had it with sex. I mean you kinda hit this hump in a relationship where it is like, 'yeah, it's whatever' and it's kinda where we are at; we aren't 20 years old and have to have sex every day."

When men who use pornography make a request of a woman they are with to mimic something they saw in pornography, the most common request is for men to have anal sex with a female partner. This often happens in the teen years. For example, 16 to 18-year-old girls and boys who had experience having male to female anal sex cited the boy's desire to re-enact what he saw in porn as the most common reason they engaged in the behavior. Girls described the experience using the terms "painful, risky, and coercive." When teens spoke about having anal sex, they normalized the behavior despite the fact that it was both painful and unsafe regarding sexually transmitted infections (STI) transmission and the potential for internal damage to the recipient.[213]

Why are More Extreme Images Needed?

A commonly referenced phenomenon with pornography use is having to seek more extreme and violent images, which once seemed too disgusting, in order to achieve the same level of arousal as when one initially looked at pornography. This was the case with Greg and others who I interviewed for this book. Dr. Bridges mentioned that users of pornography tend to slide into more and more extreme images. Through a process of habituation, images that first lead us to have a strong emotional reaction lose their punch over time as they are viewed repeatedly. To achieve the same emotional response, more and more extreme images are needed to elicit a shock response. Quite simply, Bridges reminds us that we become bored quickly.[214]

Porn and Risky Sexual Behaviors

Dr. Scott Braithwaite, an Assistant Professor of Psychology at Brigham Young University, led a series of studies about how the use of pornography affects sexual relationships. One increasingly common type of sexual relationship is referred to as 'friends with benefits.' This type of relationship is defined as being friends and engaging in sexual relations, but having no romantic or other commitment to one another. Researchers suggest that these relationships pose a high risk of contracting an STI. They have also found that the more frequently people view pornography, the more likely they are to be in a friends with benefits relationship and the risky sexual behaviors in which they engage. Importantly, they found that people who used pornography frequently and had sexual scripts that were sexually permissive were the most likely to be in friends with benefits relationships.[215]

In a related study, Dr. Braithwaite and his research team explored the phenomenon of hooking up. As differentiated from friends with benefits, hooking up involves having sexual relations with someone you do not particularly know. It is also more likely to be a one-time event rather than an occasional, repeated sexual encounter with the same person. In their research, Dr. Braithwaite's research team found that the more people used pornography, the more likely they were to hook up, and the more hookup partners they have had. Like in the case of friends with benefits relationships, they found that the relationship between pornography use and hooking up depended on the individual's sexual script. If they had a more permissive sexual script, high pornography use seemed to lead to more hook-up partners.[216] Finally, Dr. Braithwaite's research team examined the risky behaviors of consuming alcohol and the absence of condoms in a sexual encounter. They found that the more frequently college students used pornography, the more likely they were to have a penetrative hookup, while intoxicated, and without a condom. Thus in several ways, frequent use of pornography was associated with high-risk sexual behavior.[217]

Erectile Dysfunction

One of the greatest impacts that increasing pornography use is having on today's generation of teens and young adults is the sharp rise in cases of erectile dysfunction – the inability to obtain or maintain an erection during a sexual encounter. A study of heterosexual men addicted to pornography found that over 60% had erectile dysfunction with a woman, but *not* when they used pornography.[218] Clearly, this is a pervasive issue. Thus if a man is addicted to pornography, it is likely that he will be unable to function sexually with a woman.

One of the leading researchers on the connection between pornography and erectile dysfunction is Dr. Norman Doidge. Dr. Doidge is a psychiatrist who specializes in the ability of the brain to form new pathways and return to former states, also called neuroplasticity. In his work, he noticed that the male patients in his practice who viewed a lot of pornography were also reporting various forms of erectile dysfunction. His patients noted that while at first, pornography could help them get more stimulated during sex, over time, it reversed and made it more difficult for them to function with their partners. Like other researchers have found,[219] in order to maintain an erection with their sexual partner, they had to conjure up images from pornography.[220]

Increase in ED Over Time

Data on erectile dysfunction over time shows a dramatic pattern, with a massive increase after Internet pornography became widely available. The earliest data, from the late 1940s, found that less than 1% of men under 30 and less than 3% of men between 30 and 45 experienced erectile dysfunction (ED).[221] The next large-scale study was published in 1999 based on data from 1992, when print pornography was more widely available than before, but Internet pornography did not yet exist. In 1992, 7% of men age 18-29 and 9% of men age 30-39 experienced ED.[222] An important part of that study to note is the finding that men age 50-59 were over three times more likely to experience ED than men 18-29. Thus, older men experienced much more ED than younger men. Then the Internet was invented; with it came affordable and anonymous access to pornography on smaller and increasingly more portable screens. Several recent studies now show that between 26% and 33% of young men experience ED. [223] [224]

For example, a study of adolescents found that 26% had experienced erectile dysfunction.[225] Given that not all adolescents have had sexual intercourse, one would expect that the number of adolescents who have ED during a sexual encounter would be lower than for men a little older. Consistent with this logic, a study in 2012 of sexually active men between age 18 and 25 found that 30% had experienced ED.[226] In the same timeframe, in a study of men age 21-40 who were in the military, 33% had experienced erectile dysfunction.[227] In the military study, researchers noted that the rate of ED more than doubled in the military from 2004-2013.[228] Thus, over time, ED for young men went from about 2%, to about 8%, to about 30%. This has all coincided with increased access to pornography.

When medical professionals have been surveyed, they note that decades ago, almost no men under 40 complained to their doctors about ED. Today, one in four new ED patients are under the age of 40. For these young men, they lack chronic or temporary illnesses, common to older men, as an explanation for ED.[229] As evidence that this rise in ED is connected to pornography use, another study found that men who consumed pornography more than once a week had twice as high levels of ED than men who viewed pornography less than once a week.[230]

A Concluding Thought

The many ways that pornography undermines healthy sexual relationships are clear. The human impact is profound. Dr. Mary Anne Layden teaches us that pornography is an ideal learning tool, in the sense that it is effective though not desirable.[231] She notes that pornography offers all the things the brain wants in a learning experience – "images, arousal, reinforcement, and the example of others" (Layden, 2010, p. 56). She also noted that a large volume of research supports a simple conclusion, "Pornography makes violence sexy" (p. 61). By making violence sexy, pornography is rewriting the modern sexual script to make it more physically aggressive and less loving and intimate. This result can be devastating for women and, indeed, for men. Though it is inherently obvious it is worth noting that there is nothing about pornography that supports God's design for sexual relationships. In fact, pornography undermines God's design for sexual intimacy in every conceivable way.

Chapter 12

Sexual Abuse Pictures, Also Known as Child Pornography

Child pornography has become one of the largest social concerns on Earth.[232] There are fundamental ways in which child pornography is different from images that depict adults. First, it exploits a highly vulnerable and impressionable population. Obviously, child pornography involves sexual pictures of people under the age of 18, who legally cannot appear in pornographic media. While some adult pornography is illegal if it is obscene, all child pornography is legally prohibited in the United States.

Definitions are also important when discussing the present subject matter. When I interviewed Dr. Mary Anne Layden, a faculty member and psychotherapist at the University of Pennsylvania, she suggested that the term "child pornography" was not quite appropriate. She argued that we should call it "sexual abuse pictures." Because a child has been photographed in an act that they legally cannot consent to, the phrase "sexual abuse pictures" is more accurate. However, because most research and the overwhelming majority of people I interviewed referred to this as child pornography, that is the term that appears most often in this chapter.

Scope

Worldwide pornography revenues from a variety of sources total approximately $100 billion annually.[233] Child pornography is $20 billion of that, bringing in 20% of the revenue to the pornography industry.[234] As with most any business, the pornography industry has a vested interest in keeping 20% of its income intact. Research on male pornography users has found that 21% view child pornography as part of what they consume. These men are more likely than other men to be frequent viewers of pornography and to report that they enjoy new and exciting experiences. Not surprisingly, child pornography viewers are more likely than other pornography viewers to be interested in engaging in sexual behavior with an underage person.[235] Relatedly, when the sexual interests of child pornography offenders are assessed, they show more sexual arousal to children than to adults.[236]

Childification of adult pornography

Why would so many men be looking at child pornography? Aside from being a sinful matter of individual choice (which is an important reason, for which they are responsible), it also may be partly due to the efforts of the pornography industry to create more extreme forms of media that will continue to satisfy its users who seek a return to the first high they got from viewing porn. One way in which the industry is moving viewers into child content is the childification of adult pornography. In my interview with Dr. Walter DeKeseredy, author of *Violence Against Women in Pornography*, he remarked, "If you look at the content of a lot of today's pornography it is childification, taking 18 year olds and making them look like they are 14." Dr. Gail Dines, author of *Pornland: How Today's Pornography Has Hijacked our Sexuality*, noted in our recent interview

> "The industry is looking to younger and younger looking models. That is actually linking to

non-pedophile men using either teen porn, where they might be 18 or not but they look like children or at least adolescents, and how that is a gateway to men who have never used child porn, going into child porn."

This assertion is backed up by a recent report, published by the Witherspoon Institute at Princeton University, stating

"There is abundant evidence that for many pornography users, their interest in adult pornography gradually leads them into child pornography.[237] Perhaps it is the ever more popular genre of barely legal pornography and/or pornography featuring models who have (allegedly) recently turned 18 years old."

When I interviewed Tommy, an 18-year-old male who is a frequent viewer of pornography, I asked him what age he thought the youngest person he had seen in porn was. He reflected and responded,

"The youngest should be 18 but I think the youngest I've seen would probably be 15 or 14; mainly the female. It's mainly like an older adult, like a homemade video with a younger girl. It is usually almost always homemade instead of like a scene that she planned. It's mainly just the homemade stuff. Usually the guy is like 18 but not much older. It's always like a girl who doesn't really know what to do, so the male just kind of takes over and controls the whole thing. And it is kind of an innocent act for the girl. It's almost like abuse. It's like forcing her because they are so young. Mainly it is just sex. The girl is enjoying it, sometimes."

I asked Tommy if it ever wasn't something the 14-year-old girl liked. He said "Yes," and continued "Its kinda hard to watch I guess. I don't find anything like that arousing, just seeing someone in pain, clearly not enjoying it, feeling like it is abusive." What Tommy described is a video of rape recorded by a male who is of legal age to consent, with a female who either did not or cannot consent to sexual intercourse given her age. Such rape videos can be easily uploaded and shared on the Internet. These images, made without the female's consent, can never be fully eliminated from the Internet and can come back to harm her for the rest of her life.

Another of the research participants for this book who saw child pornography was Katie, a woman in her 20s who is at the tail end of completing her college degree. When I asked her the youngest person she had seen in pornography, she said, "Probably 14. They were with an older person." Katie saw this, unintentionally, when she walked into the room of a male friend.

> "We walked into one of our friend's rooms, and he had it up, and he was like trying to shut it off, so clearly you can see it when it is on your computer. Kinda awkward walking in when someone is watching porn. I thought it was kind of awkward (in the video clip) for a 14-year-old boy to be with a 30-year-old woman. It's kinda weird. It looked like it was [my friend] just went on Google and went on a porn site. Its weird. Just looking at (the 14 year old boy's) face. I mean you can tell when someone is in puberty and been through it, yeah that is what I was thinking, he looks really young to be in a porn. It was kinda one of those things you are 14 years old, I mean he may have been a little older, but he really looked 14ish." This type of pornography, where young males engage in

sexual relations with women much older than they, is growing in popularity. In fact, a term used to search for this kind of pornography was the third most common search term used in 2014 by people searching a popular website that directs people to the type of porn they wish to view.[238]

Another way that people see child pornography today is through malware or pop-ups on their computer. When I asked Taylor, a citizen of Thailand in her 30s, what the youngest person she had seen in pornography was, she responded,

> "I think a junior high person. What I've seen, they were Asian as you can see Asian people look young, but I believe they were in junior high school, probably 14 or 15. (I saw it in a) pop up. I felt bad. I feel like they shouldn't do that, they should study or do other activities. I mean it was not good for their future lives, I felt like they should do other things than that, they have tons of activities they can do like singing, playing a musical instrument, but not do this. I felt like their parents, if they see that, or even if their future husband or boyfriend saw that, it would not have been good."

Child porn will increase

The quantity of available child pornography is likely to increase in the years ahead, with the anticipated increase in such images made possible as the pornography industry will likely move its base of operation to Eastern Europe. Much of this has to do with the inner workings of the pornography industry. According to Dr. Gail Dines,

"With the movement of the porn industry to Eastern Europe, that shift is going to expand child porn on the Internet, because who can stop them? Alongside that, MindGeek has been financing the Free Speech Coalition (the lobby group for the porn industry) to basically get rid of Proposition 2257, and that is very important. The courts recently ruled against a legal challenge to 2257. 2257 wasn't struck down because if it was, it would open things up to child porn and 2257 is the only way at this moment that you can go after distributors like MindGeek who are uploading child porn."

All of this bears some explanation. Proposition 2257 is the law mandating that the pornography industry must maintain records for everyone who appears in pornography, assuring that they meet the minimum 18 years of age requirement. The lobbying group that represents the pornography industry, a group that fights to remove such regulations from pornography, calls itself the Free Speech Coalition. This group is reportedly attempting to get rid of the age requirement from appearing in pornography. The Free Speech Coalition is getting a great deal of financing from a business called MindGeek. MindGeek is an Internet company that is attempting to buy up as many free pornography websites as possible, so that they can make money from it – either through advertising or by making the site a paid site. MindGeek appears to be including a good deal of child pornography on their website, and therefore has a vested interest in getting rid of the laws against child pornography; thus their financing of the pro-child pornography group, The Free Speech Coalition.

Difference between child porn only users and "contact" sex offenders

When scholars study people who view child pornography, many of them divide them into three categories – those who look at child pornography but do not act out on it with a child, those who look at child pornography and have a "contact offense" with a child, and those who do not look at child pornography but have a contact offense with a child. A contact offense involves sexually touching a child.

When researchers compare the characteristics of people who possess online child pornography, child sex offenders, and people who both possess child pornography and are child sex offenders, numerous differences are apparent. A review of 30 studies found that child sex offenders were more likely to have access to children than were men who only looked at child pornography. In a similar way, those who were online child pornography only offenders had more access to the Internet than contact offenders. Compared to child pornography only offenders, contact sex offenders and those who had both child pornography and had committed a contact sex offense were more likely to be antisocial. Like other types of sex offenders, contact sex offenders had low empathy for victims. Based on a review of 30 studies, researchers determined that contact sex offenders who also possessed child pornography committed the most sex offenses with children.[239]

CP arrestees likely to also be contact offenders

Scholars have discovered several things about the behavior of men who use child pornography. For example, if a man is arrested for child pornography (a small minority of child porn viewers who likely were also involved in distribution), there is a greater than 50% chance that he has sexually abused a child. Most have several victims.[240] The characteristics of men who use child pornography that are associated with a higher likelihood that they have had a contact offense include having younger children and more extreme content featured in confiscated pornography.[241]

Dr. Drew Kingston of the University of Ottawa studied contact offenders. He and his research team found that if a man had been arrested for contact offense, he is more likely to be arrested a second time if he used pornography frequently and if that pornography was more deviant.[242] Another risk factor for reoffending, found by Dr. Michael Seto and his research team, is having committed another crime in the past.[243]

Soliciting children on Internet

In so many ways, the Internet changed the scope of the pornography business; bringing it to more people in an affordable and accessible way as well as allowing increasingly anonymous ways of viewing. One way that technological changes impacted pornography in general and child abuse in particular is through soliciting children for sex over the Internet. Between 1998, when the Internet was in its infancy and 2006, when the Internet was ubiquitous, there was a 400% increase in the number of children who were being solicited for sexual reasons over the Internet. These solicitations include chatting and getting a child to take clothes off, or having the adult expose himself to a child in front of a webcam.[244] During the same time frame, there was an over 2,000% increase in investigations and 1,300% increase in convictions of men who were exchanging sexual images with children online.[245] Many of these convictions come from undercover agents who pose as children online in order to catch sexual predators.

Arrests Up Due To Sexting

Another phenomenon that has led to an increase in arrests for child pornography is the act of "sexting" or taking and sharing a picture of oneself naked or partly naked. Many teens are doing this through their cell phones and web cams. In fact, when researchers studied the sexting behavior of high school students, they found that 28% had ever sent a naked picture of themselves to someone else at some point. About the same number, 31%, requested a naked picture from someone else. Many more, 57% had been asked to send a sext message, thus indicating that over half of teens asked for a sext turn the request down. High school students who have sexted are much more likely to be sexually active. Girls who sexted, in addition to being more likely to have had sex, are also more likely to have engaged in risky sexual practices, such as not using safer sex practices.[246]

With the dramatic rise in adolescents who are given their own phones and those who have webcams on their computers, the possibility for sexting has increased dramatically. Arrests for sexting-related offenses went up 500% from 2000 to 2009. This rise in arrests, at first blush, could lead to the conclusion that innocent teenagers are being wrongfully arrested for sending photos of themselves in bathing suits to a romantic partner. To the contrary, in most of these arrests, an adult enticed a minor to take a picture of themself and send it to (usually) him; and it was the adult who was arrested.[247] Most people who were arrested were White males. Not many had arrest records. Most of the offenders also had pornographic pictures in their possession of preteen children being sexually abused. Throughout this decade of the new millennium, the proportion of offenders who were 18-25 years old increased.[248]

Context for sexting

When researchers have looked deeply into cases of sexting where police were involved in some way, most of the time either an adult solicited an image (36% of the time) or an underage person sent a sexting image of someone else, where there was either a lack of consent or malicious intent (31%). When adults were involved, about two thirds of cases resulted in an arrest. When youth were the only ones involved and there was either lack of consent or malicious intent, about a third of the time there was an arrest. In cases where youth were involved and the police determined that there was no malicious intent, about one in six cases resulted in arrest. In the majority of cases, pictures were sent through cell phones. Very rarely did someone who sent a sext message end up on the sex offender registry.[249]

Joe's Story

The story of my interview with "Joe" is unlike any other in this book; it is perhaps the most disturbing. I will share in substantially more detail than others. Joe did time in jail for possession and distribution of child pornography. There is a lot we can learn from his experience, both from his experience and how his church family responded. I do caution you, the reader. I do not censor what he told me here, and some of what he recounted was graphic. If you think it could be upsetting to you, I suggest that you skip reading this section.

I drove to Joe's home to meet with him in person for an interview. As I drove to his house, located just outside a major metropolitan area of the United States, I followed the directions of my GPS device and was surprised to find myself on unpaved dirt roads, still at least a mile from his house. I passed several run down trailers and old, small homes before arriving at his house. Along the dirt road I passed two different signs that read "children playing." I couldn't block the thought that this might not be the best place for someone convicted for child pornography offenses to live.

The location was far from any school, park, or day care center – as required by Joe's jail sentence. Knowing that his house was a little difficult to find, Joe stood in the front yard to wave so I would know that I had found the right place. I was a little uneasy driving up to his house. Although I had met convicted sex offenders before, I had never visit the home of one. I didn't quite know what to expect. I got out of my car and walked through his front yard, and was greeted by a jubilant dog – not a guard dog; the most she might do is lick you to death. I was struck by the fact that Joe didn't say anything to me as I walked up his extended front yard toward his house. After waving me down, he left me with the dog, turned around and started to head back into the house. He waited until I got inside to say hello. He was obviously very nervous about what we were going to talk about. He offered me coffee and we found a place to sit.

After noticing that he was very nervous, the next thing that struck me was his obvious psychological pain. He came across as being deeply troubled by what he had done. I point that out not to make any excuses for him, but rather to convey the remorse I could feel from his demeanor. Joe is in his late 60s, but appeared to be in his late 70s. His face showed his age. Oddly, not a single light was on in the house, so far as I could tell, and it remained that way throughout our interview. The power wasn't out, so I took the lack of light as Joe's choice. It struck me as symbolic. We could see reasonably well with natural light shining in from a couple windows, but it was noticeably dark. I couldn't help but feel Joe's hesitation to be seen too clearly.

Joe seemed forthcoming for much of the interview. He was most hesitant to talk about prior contact offenses and the exact types of pictures he downloaded from the Internet, yet he left little room for imagination when pressed. I asked him when he first saw something one would consider pornographic. He responded,

> "I got started in pornography when I was 10 or 11 years old. We were going to an amusement park and they had a girlie show box there. We would put a dime in and see it and that is the first time I saw any pornography. It's a little box with a movie thing in it, you put a dime in it, it plays a movie, there is some girl stripping in it."

Like many males in his generation, and those to come, he next moved on to *Playboy Magazine*.

> "I'd buy the Playboy magazines once in a while. I don't think I was addicted to pornography but I was a healthy male, the female form was the biggest mystery in the world (laughs), still is! Anyway so it wasn't really a battle or anything like that. Then the Internet came along and man I mean it was everywhere on there. I got to messing in that. And I, I'm thoroughly ashamed of it, and before I know it I was addicted."

Joe was not at all hesitant to use the word addicted. In describing his experience, he knew that is when he was thoroughly hooked. He noted,

> "My wife knew I was dabbling in that and she said 'Oh you need help' but I said 'Oh I can quit that whenever I want to.' I've heard that any addict, they feel they can quit anytime they want to. And I didn't feel like I needed help or anything so anyway, I started downloading songs. I love old music from

the 1940s and stuff like that and that place I was downloading the songs, there was some ad for young models or something like that and I clicked on it and it was the child pornography stuff. And I got to watching that."

It is noteworthy that Joe didn't initially seek out child pornography. He saw an ad for young models, clicked on it, and fell into a deep chasm of sin. Joe spoke of how difficult it was to break his addiction. In fact, he said it was impossible without help.

"So it is a struggle. I would like to wipe it completely out, but I don't know how you do that. I mean if you are a man, it is going to turn you on. To me it is. I don't know. I've been around men all my life and most of them I know it is about the same with them."

He then spoke in more detail about the images he began to seek out.

"I don't know what other people think, but the breast part of women is one, everybody they say has a specialty, they like the butt or the breast or the feet. So anyway, I think it was the forming of the breast on the young kids that attracted me. I don't know. That seemed to be the one thing I wanted to see when I get on there. I feel terrible, I feel terrible talking about this like this OK, (he laughed nervously). But to know why I did it, I think I have to face the truth on why I did do it. So that is the only thing I can come up with and I'm doing everything I can to keep that from ever happening again."

Before Joe had access to the Internet, he occasionally watched HBO movies or other types of what some might call 'soft porn.' He noted,

> "Once in a while there would be something on TV and I would watch that, just knowing there is going to be some nudity in it, like HBO. Now we didn't subscribe to that a lot but there was times that ... they will throw some free stuff in there to try to entice you to buy it and they still do it, so it was more stuff like that than actually subscribing to it. Anytime there was something in there like that I'd try to slip around and watch it."

Joe also described visiting an occasional strip club, before he ever had access to the Internet.

> "There many years ago I used to slip away to a nudie bar once in a while, stuff like that. I wouldn't tell my wife of course. They had adult theaters, there was a time or two I'd slip off and go to one of those or something. It was pretty raw. I didn't do that pretty often but I have done it but that was kind of it."

Joe talked about the impact his pornography use had on him,

> "I wasted a huge amount of time. My wife was getting ready to leave me (he cried). Actually there was a lot of good coming out of me getting caught. My wife was going to leave me, and I don't blame her. My kids didn't know that stuff was going on but they knew my wife was unhappy. And I've got 4 beautiful daughters, my granddaughters are grown they are beautiful, and they love me, but

(he cries) that's what makes it hurt so bad, I've got
a beautiful family. And I've stained them (he cried
again). My wife should have left me and if I hadn't
got caught she probably would have been gone by
now or thrown me out or something. So there was
some good come out of this."

Joe's computer was in a part of the house that his family didn't tend
to go.

"The computer was upstairs. A desktop. The first
computer we got was a telephone thing [dial up
Internet], and so slow to download a picture, took
you 30 minutes. I didn't know anything about
computers; it took a while to get into that. And like
I say I was downloading the songs, and it was some
kind of share group. It was where people who have
stuff on their computers, you can access what you
got on their computers, that is one of the things they
convicted me on was the sharing stuff. To me it was
all Internet, I didn't know. Anyway, so if they had
that stuff on their computer you could download
it on to yours. They could access my computer too
through that sharing group and that is what they
got me on (referencing his arrest). I would download
it (pornography) on CDs and stuff like that."

Joe noted that he stopped and started viewing child pornography
several times. One of the things that would get him to stop,
temporarily, was his pastor.

"(My pastor) had preached something at church and
I'd come home, destroy all that, clean that computer
up, say this ain't never going to happen again. The

next thing I would know something would come up and I'd be back up there again. It would be worse than it was before. There is something spiritual about a demon being swept out of the house and he comes back and it was worse than it was before; that is the way it was for me."

Joe talked about the process of downloading images.

"You couldn't actually tell what you were downloading until you downloaded. You couldn't see it, so all you had to go by was their description and they had a description for everything. Not a detailed description, so you downloaded some stuff that was pretty gross and I would delete it immediately, I hate telling you this ... It was actually the forming of the boobs is what I was looking at, okay? I don't know."

Joe was deeply embarrassed to make the admission. After a while of viewing child pornography, he was caught in a sting organized by the U.S. Secret Service.

"Now there was some stuff on my computer that had downloaded, I'm quite sure that the feds had a lot to do with what was downloaded on that computer because it would usually take a week or two for that to download; the other stuff (from the Secret Service) downloaded within an hour, (which was the day) before they arrested me. They were fixin' to do something, and it was stuff I normally wouldn't look at."

I asked Joe what it was that was on his computer. It was a topic he clearly did not want to go very deeply into.

> "They had boobs. If they didn't have boobs I didn't even look at it, I'd just delete it. I didn't like (pictures of intercourse with children) either. It was more, I don't know, I don't want to get into that too much. I wasn't looking for that part of it (adult/child intercourse). In fact, that grossed me out. I wondered where is their Daddy? Why is that happening? What is going on with this? I would have loved to have helped them, I didn't know how."

Despite his being elderly and physically frail, he was arrested by a swat team in the middle of the night.

> "They sent a swat team to my house, broke the back door down, my wife and I were asleep and I woke up to my wife asking 'Who are you?' They were screaming at her 'Get on the floor!!' And that is what I heard and I jumped out of bed and ran into the kitchen there and my wife was backed into a corner there and they had red dots all over her chest from the rifles and I didn't' know what was going on, and I thought what am I doing? I was going to jump right into them, there was about 5 of them so I was going to jump right on top of them because I didn't know what else to do! I didn't have a gun or weapon or anything. And I didn't know who they were, they were kind of crouching and they had all the night vision stuff on and I was just going to jump on them because I didn't know who they were. One stood up and he was fixin' to pull the trigger. I thought if they start shooting they are

going to shoot (my wife) so I backed down but I was touching his rifle when I stopped. I didn't know what to do."

Although Joe was shocked when he got out of bed to a swat team, he knew exactly why they were there.

"They had us handcuffed and sitting on the floor in there. I said 'well aren't you some big brave people, you are afraid of us! You are this afraid of us!' It was my fault, I shouldn't have been doing what I been doing and I understand that."

There were two prosecutors on site with the swat team along with members of the Secret Service. Joe continued,

"I thought well 'my goodness what is the Secret Service doing here?' They took us out to the vehicles in the driveway, my wife in one, me in the other. They told me that I was looking at hundreds of thousands of dollars of fines and 10 to 20 years in prison. He said 'If you'll cooperate with us and be truthful, we know the county prosecutor personally and we can get this reduced for you if you will cooperate and tell the truth.' They gave me this big long spiel about telling the truth and you ain't no kind of man if you don't tell the truth and all that. I mean it was a five-minute speech they give me about that, so they asked me if I ever had touched anyone. I told that woman (a prosecutor) that I had touched a niece oh 50 years ago. And she had come to me later and talked to me about it and I told her, man that wasn't your fault. I was the one who should have been protecting you from that. And it was, we"

> were sitting on the couch, and got to tickling each
> other and I tickled her ..."

Joe wouldn't continue that story at that point. My sense was that
he touched the breasts of his niece, but he didn't explicitly say that.
After giving a brief statement, they took Joe to jail.

> "They didn't do anything to my wife, they were
> threatening to arrest her as an accessory. My wife
> knew I was into porn; she didn't know I was in to
> child porn and I think they finally believed her.
> But they didn't take her, she didn't leave the house
> or anything. And that would have devastated me if
> they had done anything to that woman."

Once they took Joe to jail, a district attorney interviewed him.

> "They took me to the jail and the DA had an office
> there and they were going to give me a lie detector
> test. They were asking me all kinds of terrible
> things. Have you ever done this. I mean I'm not
> even going to tell you what they were telling me.
> And I told that prosecutor. He gave me the same
> spiel that the other guy, the other one did, the one
> who gave me a lie detector test. How he knew the
> DA and they were personal friends and if you would
> just be truthful and cooperative we will help you get
> out of this so anyway he gave me a lie detector test.
> He said, 'Well you failed this lie detector test.' He
> said 'There is something you are not telling me.' He
> said 'Have you ever inappropriately touched any of
> your daughters or anything.' I had thought about it,
> we had bought my oldest daughter a motorcycle and
> my youngest daughter was about 15 and she wanted

to drive it and she drove it around the yard a little. And then she wanted to get out on the road. And my wife said you can't get out there unless your dad goes with you. So I got on the motorcycle behind her and she took off and I grabbed her boobs. Cause I was hanging on for life. And I told that guy I felt embarrassed that I grabbed her boobs. And he said well did you touch her nipples? And I said well probably, (he laughed nervously). I touched her, but it was an accident and I told him it was an accident but then as soon as I told him that, the DA's office was right next to that room, and I could hear everything next door. He ran, I mean he ran in there and yelled 'I got him to admit that he molested his daughter!' Like he scored a touchdown at the high school game. And there wasn't nothing about how cooperative he was, or be lenient. Then I knew I'd been had. I have no respect for any law enforcement now, I promise you. And I didn't get an attorney (at the time), they give me the rights thing and I knew I was guilty and I didn't see what an attorney, I didn't know an attorney, I didn't know how to get an attorney, so I waived my rights to an attorney."

Joe noted that he asked his daughter about this incident, now about 30 years later.

"After this happened, we asked my daughter about it and she didn't even remember it. They said I had incestuous tendencies, which is the reason I felt guilty about touching her. That is what the Secret Service said. They had a profiler say that is why he felt guilty."

When I interviewed Joe, it was difficult to tell how he asked his daughter about the incident years ago, and whether she really didn't remember or didn't want to talk about it. As Joe was being interviewed in jail and the lie detector administrator and the DA were talking, he continued to listen through the wall.

> "I knew I'd been had after he ran in there and told that DA that. The DA said well he is dirty, book him, I heard all that. I don't think they knew I could hear them. Maybe they don't care. In fact, when they had the charges against me that they give to the judge, give a copy of it to me, they had written, the feds had written on there for what he's done, and what we think he might have done, we think he deserves jail time and it should be extensive jail time. It wasn't 'be lenient' or anything like that. Now my only consolation in that is that God is looking at all this and he knows what they are doing. Not only does he know what I was doing he knows what they were doing. And they are going to pay for that. I am bitter, I've tried to forgive that, but that is tough. I am going through so much right now that I'm trying to process, I'm still trying to process that. I've been out six months. I was in jail five months; it was a 6-month term. That was an eye opener too. Just being in jail! That's an experience."

While waiting for his arraignment in jail, Joe was about to kill himself. He recalled,

> "If I was going to spend 10 years ... we've got a little bit of savings and that was going to wipe us out. Here (my wife) would be stuck with me in jail and her broke. And that pretty well devastated me just

thinking about that. So I was going to kill myself. That was the only way I could see out of that ... I think my wife had figured I was planning something."

Joe's wife got him an attorney, who was able to get him released on a bond. He noted that his church family came to his bond hearing, about a dozen of them, and put together the funds to pay the bond and for his attorney.

Joe noted that he never took pictures of a child; he did have many pictures taken by others on his computer. He was convicted for possession of child pornography and Internet crimes for sharing files of the pictures he downloaded.

When Joe was sentenced, the judge told him "You are the reason that stuff is on the Internet. You offend every fiber of my being." I could tell that the rationale that the judge gave to Joe, though based in sound logic, did not register with Joe. He wasn't able to see that if people stopped downloading child pornography, there would be no incentive for others to upload it. Joe was sentenced to serve 6 months in jail. When he told me that was his sentence, I was actually surprised the term was that short. He also now registers as a sex offender, and cannot go near a school, park, or day care center. He is also banned from going on the Internet.

After being in jail, Joe was no longer able to work in a small business he owned. His wife had to go back to work in a restaurant, to supplement Joe's social security. He noted,

> "I feel a failure for not being able to provide like I should, so far we are getting by. That hurts to see my wife struggling so. My wife is a saint, if it wasn't for her I'd be dead, I'd have killed myself by now." Joe meant it.

I asked Joe for the advice he would share with others. He said,

> "Don't get started in porn; even if it is not illegal it is
> still bad. Unless you are really deviated I don't think
> you'd get into child porn if you didn't get into porn
> first. Porn is bad enough in itself. I never thought of
> it being an addiction like drugs, but it is; something
> about the chemicals in the brain or something. They
> say it is harder to get rid of that than drug addiction.
> If you are doing anything that would make you go
> back to looking at child porn, what led you there
> if you are starting that over, you could be led right
> back again. So even looking at the bikini movies
> can be a path back, so I've had to guard against that
> by just not doing it. The Internet is going to be a
> terrible thing, terrible! What if I was 18 and it got
> attached to me, it would ruin your life. Ruin it! And
> there is lots of kids like that now. I'm old and don't
> have much longer to go right now anyways. It is not
> as devastating for me as it is for someone 18 years
> old; that would cause suicides if you had to live with
> this the rest of your lives. I never want to get back
> into that. It has freed me up so much. I have more
> time than I ever had before. That Internet consumed
> me, you'd get on the Internet and you'd be on there
> 4 hours and it would seem like 10 minutes. I'm
> free from all that pornography stuff (now) … If I
> can help somebody get off that; don't start to start
> with, just stay out of that pornography stuff. That
> is such a dead end thing, no good can come out of
> it." He continued, "The dangers of pornography,
> child pornography is one of them, that is cheating
> on your wife! You could lose your wife over it; that is
> a big danger. They know you are cheating on them.

It can't fulfill anything; you can't have the proper kind of relationship with your wife if you are doing that stuff, you can't do it. OK? It is not good for you, it's a waste of time especially if you get consumed by it like I was, if you are spending 4-5 hours a day looking at it, you are consumed by it, stop it! If you are doing it that much, you are addicted and you need help, get help! That is something else I would say; get help! Talk to your preacher, your counselor, or somebody who has been through it. I'd try to lead them to somebody like my counselor. I could tell them what has happened to me and what could happen to them – they could drive a wedge between them and the wives. Most of their wives know. You can't love your wives like you should when you are doing that because you are looking for something else. My wife is the perfect person for me. I tried to look at every woman in the world and none of them is as good as what I got."

I asked Joe how he'd suggest convincing a 16-year-old boy not to look at pornography. He replied, "You can't! I don't even know if telling them about jail would help. Having stuff that is so accessible. I mean 'you want to see me naked, click here!'"

Joe looks at his being caught as something that made a huge, positive change in his life.

"To be free of that and to have my wife love me and to love her like I do. I almost wish it had happened years ago. I should have paid more attention to her. I almost lost her. I'd be dead if I lost her. She's my whole life. I didn't realize how much she was. We've been married over 50 years."

I asked Joe if he had any advice for his faith community. He said, "Be sure to know that you know that you are a Christian, that you have turned your life over to Him (Jesus) completely. If you are looking at this stuff, you haven't turned over your life completely."

I asked Joe to reflect on why he thought he had used pornography. He recalled,

> "I used to blame this on my wife, my wife and I don't' have the sex we used to because we are old and I blamed that on her some to her face, even why I was doing pornography, yeah, she had every right to never see me again but instead she bolted to the front and got me out of there. She is an amazing woman. I'd be living in a dirty dump if it wasn't for her. I didn't realize what I had. In jail I found out I'm an invalid without her. It jolted me to realizing what I had. I wish I had that awakening with less consequences, but sometimes it takes the consequences to wake up. Don't make the Lord bring this all on you for him to straighten you up. I was at the pit, ready to end it all, I didn't see any way out of it. I'm still on parole, if I step out of line any way, I could go back to jail."

A Concluding Thought

This chapter was likely among the most difficult for you to read. Few, aside from those in the pornography industry itself, would argue that it is acceptable to make pornography with children and adolescents. It is also deeply disturbing to know that people who are not yet legally capable of giving consent to sexual behavior are being forced to submit to a wide variety of behaviors. We can be certain that most children involved in pornography have experienced tremendous, lifelong, trauma from their involvement. In today's age of the Internet, their images can never fully be taken back. With new technologies come new ways of abusing children, and recording the acts. It us up to every individual, and every parent, to do all they can to avoid viewing such images, stop those who are making the images from doing so, and diminish the demand for pictures of child abuse. Our world's children depend upon our efforts. If you or someone you know has been affected some way by child pornography, I encourage you to contact your pastor, the National Center for Missing and Exploiting Children, or a Christian counselor.

Chapter 13

What Can I Do? Confronting Pornography in Your Life, The Lives of Others, and in our Society

"This is a public health crisis like we have never seen before. There has been a massive dereliction on the part of adults to take this seriously, and by doing that, they have handed their kids over to the porn industry." -- Dr. Gail Dines.

Those of us who have a Christian worldview rightly see the problem of pornography as primarily a sin issue. It is also more than that. The Christian faith has many sufficient reasons to claim that pornography is a cancer on the soul. In order to fight the battle on a broader societal level, I also believe we need to understand the ways in which pornography is a public health issue.

The degree to which pornography has become extremely violent, universally available, and used by so many is a public health crisis. It is also apparent that many adults have not taken this seriously, nor have they helped their children navigate around these landmines. Indeed many parents have been caught off guard by the menacing nature of today's pornography. Please don't be one of them.

If you are a parent, a pastor, or might be one someday, you need to understand how the pornography industry wants to make children addicted to pornography for their profits. All of us, parents, pastors, teenagers, grandparents, concerned citizens, academics, scholars, writers, legislators, religious leaders and those in the secular community can do something to attenuate the impact of pornography. It may be in our own lives, the lives of others, or being involved in a broader societal change.

In this chapter, I will briefly review some of the reasons why people and our society at large need to address the issue of pornography. Then, I will offer ideas for taking action. I will talk about ways that people can stop using pornography. Next, I will offer suggestions for how you as a friend, parent, grandparent, pastor, or other person concerned with another's wellbeing, can help bring people into a lifestyle that is free from pornography. Finally, I will offer some advice on how we can work together to make societal change in this sphere.

Why Bother?

Pornography is addictive.[250] Among many other harms, this is high on the list of the most dangerous. Not all who view pornography will become addicted, just as not all who smoke cigarettes will become addicted to nicotine. However, pornography has been shown by many renowned scholars to have addictive properties. Psychiatrists tend to define addiction occurring when three of the following things are present in the past year: 1) the development of tolerance, 2) withdrawal symptoms, 3) loss of control, 4) attempts to cut down, 5) significant time spent thinking about or obtaining that which one is addicted to, and 6) reduced involvement in social, work, or recreation activities.[251] These symptoms describe the experience of several men interviewed for this book. They also are consistent with available scholarship. For example, the most common problem associated with Internet use is Internet sexual addiction, often involving pornography and adult chat rooms used for sexual experiences producing negative consequences.[252][253] People who have pornography addiction can spend as much as 35 to 45 hours per week on the Internet.[254]

A key body of literature demonstrating that pornography is addictive comes from neuroscience. In a comprehensive report about the available studies on pornography and addictive responses in the brain, a team of researchers found that people who are addicted to online pornography have virtually the same neural processes occur in the brain as those addicted to illicit drugs. When you compare the widely accepted definition of an addiction from the American Psychiatric Association to symptoms experienced by compulsive pornography users, Internet pornography addiction is clearly a neurological addiction.[255]

Another reason we should be concerned about pornography was raised by in my interview with Dr. Paul Wright from Indiana University. He noted with trepidation,

> "We still have no idea about the long term implications of the Internet pornography boom. We can only speculate. My students are constantly pointing out to me kinds of pornography I've never heard of. I think the possibility of a cultural, global sea change in sexuality and people's sexual scripts and templates from this availability of anything and everything, I think that is yet to be known, the scope of it; but it will change things that we can't predict."

In my interview with Dr. Mary Anne Layden from the University of Pennsylvania, she observed

"We've got to wake up, we've got to take action, we've got to work together, the mental health field needs to be taking action, the legal people need to be having lawsuits against this, the reporters need to write articles, the academics need to write books, we need everybody together, the people who are treating need to treat and we have got to get the Congress and state legislatures to pass laws. And we have got to have the will of the people, we've got to convince the DSM to put it in there."

Dr. Layden's reference to the DSM, the Diagnostic and Statistical Manual of Mental Disorders, refers to absence of pornography addiction being listed among mental illnesses by the American Psychiatric Association. Though the DSM recognizes gambling addiction, it does not yet identify pornography addiction as a problem worth treating. Scholars and therapists hope that the next revision will include this important diagnosis, so that treatment of it will be more readily accomplished.

In my recent interview with Forest Benedict, a licensed marriage and family therapist and certified sexual addiction treatment provider, he noted that

"One significant downside to the DSM not recognizing pornography addiction as a real disorder is that as the influx of addicted adolescents seek specialized treatment, these services will not be covered by their parent's insurances. As a therapist who works with porn addicted teenagers, I believe this will be detrimental to many."

Initial Steps

As I have researched this book, there are five general ideas that stand out as recommendations to people who are trying to cut down on or eliminate their own pornography use, or the use of someone they care about. These are some initial ideas:

Restrict Access

First, everyone should do everything possible to restrict online access to pornography, whether they think they want to see it or not. Some simple things one can do include setting your Internet browser to a safe setting. For example, Google has a "safe search" setting that screens out most (but not all) adult content. This feature can also be locked, so parents can set a password to insure that computers or other devices belonging to their children have at least one filter in place. To access this filter, simply go to the Google home page, go to the settings section (at the time this book was published it is in the bottom right corner of your screen), then click search settings, and click the box "turn on safe search." One of the greatest benefits of this feature is that it will help the user avoid unintentional contact with images that could lead the user to click on more extreme images. I recommend that if you have not yet done so, you put this book down, do it, and then keep reading.

Filtering and Accountability Software

Second, install an Internet filter and accountability system on all of your devices that can access the Internet. There are at least a dozen such services. The most commonly used is Covenant Eyes. One I have heard from pornography addicts that they say is the toughest to get around is called Safe Eyes. You can find them easily on the Internet. Installing accountability software, and having a parent or close friend set the password for it, will help keep explicit images and content from appearing as a result of Internet searches. It also sends a list of questionable websites to an individual designated by the owner of the Internet accessible device. If you are inclined to allow your child under 18 to have a smart phone (which I recommend against), an Internet filter and accountability system is absolutely necessary. Go through the easy set up process to have an email sent to you with a list of questionable websites they have accessed. If you have ever accessed pornography from a computer or smart phone, you too should get an Internet filtering and accountability system. Make sure an email is sent to your spouse, grandmother, accountability partner, or anyone you really wouldn't want knowing that you viewed pornography. Greg noted how Safe Eyes helped him. "I had software on my computer at that point that was very hard to get around, it was Safe Eyes, it blocked pornographic content and reported your activities to an accountability partner. So, my use was way less frequent."

As this book went to press, an app was being released by the college ministry group, StuMo (www.stumo.org). The app is called KeepR. KeepR is a basket of technologies, starting with an Android-based app which becomes the only browser and controls which apps are usable. KeepR does not monitor specific internet use, but removes images and videos – except on popular sites which are informative and/or entertaining. KeepR filters the distracting media from these popular sites. For security, KeepR tracks the phone status and reports unusual events (safe mode access, airplane mode, etc.) to the client's "shepherd" for accountability purposes. The shepherd is a trusted friend, or a parent in the case of minors. When certain images or videos are critical for professional use, KeepR gives access and reports the use. I encourage you to search for it, and when it becomes available, to install it on your devices.

Cut off your hand

Third, if you or someone you care about has a pattern of accessing explicit content on a computer or mobile device, get rid of the device. Jesus himself said in Mark 9:43 "And if your hand causes you to sin, cut it off. It is better for you to enter life crippled than with two hands to go to hell, to the unquenchable fire." Though this exhortation was likely figurative, it raises a critical point. If you are using a device to access pornography, you've tried stopping and don't, get rid of the device from which you access pornography. Thus, if something far less important than your hand causes you to sin, it is time to get rid of it. In a world where smart phones and laptops seem universal, this suggestion can seem extreme. However, given the documented effects of a pornography addiction, it is much less unpleasant to get rid of a device than it is to suffer the consequences of addictive use. As you consider this suggestion, ask yourself, "Is it safe for an alcoholic to work in a liquor store? If someone is trying to break an addiction to prescription drugs, should they work in a pharmacy?" The obvious answer to both of these questions is no. Of course, if someone has a mobile Internet device in their pocket, there is little between them and their next hit of pornography.

Get Help

Fourth, seek the assistance of someone who is experienced helping people change their behavior. I highly recommend talking with a Christian counselor who is a certified sex addiction therapist. This kind of individual can guide you through the process of overcoming an addiction or other kind of problematic use of pornography that you wish to move beyond. The process of getting this kind of support can also be helped by reading any number of books; discussed later in this chapter.

Greg talked about the importance of getting help from someone with experience. He noted that when he finally sought help from an organization called Pure Life Ministries, he was able to make progress. He shared,

> "During that period, I would talk to a counselor 30 minutes every week on the phone and tell him how my week had gone and just kind of have accountability and the for the first time in my life. I experienced a lot of freedom from that. I remember going porn free from February to May, then at the end of the semester going home, I fell back into pornography and masturbation. This was the end of freshman year. I went to a summer Christian service program with a bunch of people, it is called Kaleo, and is the summer project of Student Mobilization. I had 4 roommates; that was also a time of freedom from pornography. That marks a turning point in my fight against it. So I've still fought with it, I still do, but the nature of it is different. I think one of the main differences is that I can talk about it now and that is key just in terms of practically resisting, and having friends in the know and they can help me. So I was clean that summer."

When I interviewed Dr. William Struthers, author of *Wired for Intimacy: How Pornography Hijacks the Male Brian* and Professor of Psychology at Wheaton College, he recommended that if you need counseling for pornography use that you seek out a certified sex addiction specialist. If you are unable to find such an individual, he suggests that you find someone who specializes in sex addictions. He noted that each person needs to figure out why he is using pornography and work with a counselor on how to understand that use and overcome it.

Paul, whom we have heard from throughout this book, gave advice as someone who has a Christian worldview and was addicted to pornography for years. He has now been free from it for two years and counting. He suggested,

> "don't think that you can do it on your own because you can't, it is not possible that you could stop on your own, you can't set a goal like 'I'm not going to masturbate and watch porn for a month' it is not going to happen. You are going to break that little rule or whatever. I would say you definitely have to come to a point where, drop your pride, drop anything that is holding you back from telling somebody, get somebody that can hold you accountable and then, the number one thing would be from my Christian standpoint, you need to let go and give it up to Jesus. It is really hard to put it into words, but get on a track where you are building that relationship with Jesus and that is more important than your porn life. The biggest thing is that you can't do it on your own. There is no way."

Accountability Partner

Fifth, develop a support system, preferably a close friend or two who will hold you accountable. Often called an "accountability partner," this individual should know or be getting to know you very well, love you enough to speak unvarnished truth to you, and be someone you don't want to let down. Greg, a man we have met throughout this book, noted that in times when he has had an accountability partner, he has seen more victory than defeat. He noted,

> "It helps a lot. It keeps you from wallowing and staying there, because they are going to ask me

about it; it usually helps." In addition to having an accountability partner, Greg noted that he had a support group that helped tremendously. As he related, during his college years "an organic community began to develop in my Christian friend groups and we would meet in the basement of my house with a couple roommates and some guys from my fraternity and we read books, we confessed sin, and we would pray for each other. We would be really, completely honest about looking at pornography, masturbating, and anything. That changed the game, … we read a book … called *Samson and the Pirate Monks* by Nate Larkin, a pastor who was addicted to pornography … it is a story of redemption, people in the church came alongside him. They did one thing, they called it the Paul and Silas deal, talk to someone every day. They would just talk, how has your day been, how do you feel? Have you looked at pornography or not? So that helped a lot, we started doing that, another friend and I. We continued doing that even after I graduated, and I moved back home with my parents and for the first year we talked every day."

Recovery Programs

If someone is addicted to pornography, they will likely need a multi-pronged approach. Following the five steps I enumerated above is a good start – all of them. As a Christian, I highly value faith-based approaches to overcoming struggles with pornography. That said, I hope that many people who are not Christians are reading this book – if that is you, thank you for reading! Here are some suggestions for those who prefer a faith-based approach, and for those who do not.

The most promising non-religious program I know of to treat problematic pornography use is called The Fortify Program. It can be found at fortifyprogram.org. The Fortify program has an ongoing treatment plan and is financially accessible (it is free for those under 18 and as of the publication date of this book is only $39 for those over 18). It is designed to help people, especially young people, gain freedom from pornography use. It takes between 2 and 5 months to successfully complete online. The Fortify Program was developed by a group that has a very popular anti-porn website, Fight the New Drug. The program was written with oversight from psychologists, neurologists, therapists, and a wide variety of mental health professionals. For a very new program, they have impressive data demonstrating effectiveness. The makers of the Fortify Program shared that data with me. They note that approximately 25,000 people (mostly teens, mostly males) have participated in the program thus far. Of those people, 95% say that the program is moving them toward complete freedom from pornography. At the beginning of the program, 57% report symptoms of depression; at the end it is only 9%. The average program participant views porn 4 times per week as they start; this levels to an average of 1 time per week after a couple months. Clearly, the Fortify program is showing strong early signs of success; I recommend it highly. I also think it can be used alongside a faith based approach, making it a versatile choice for those whose pornography use is beyond their control.

A Christian-based program that I have heard a great deal about, and I support, is Celebrate Recovery (www.celebraterecovery.com). This ministry originally started at Saddleback Church. It meets in churches and other locations across the United States. These groups have a mission of helping people overcome hurts, habits, and hangups – one of which may be pornography. The program applies the Bible, with an emphasis on the beatitudes, to promote recovery. It has a 25-year history; from what I hear from participants, it is a strong program. If you do an Internet search for "Celebrate Recovery" along with the name of the place you live, there is a good chance you can find a group nearby.

Lately, I keep hearing about more promising and successful recovery programs. I will discuss new ones I hear about on videos on my website, www.johnfoubert.com. I encourage you to check them out for recent ideas.

Books I Recommend

The book that I've heard the most about in recent times that has helped people leave pornography behind is *Pure Desire* by Ted Roberts.[256] Many men whom I deeply respect have recommended this Christian book. After hearing of the life changing impact it had on them, I read it. I was very impressed, particularly by the accompanying *Seven Pillars Workbook*. The workbook is a great resource for a group working together that are looking to fight the spiritual battle against sexual impurity. The author offers an unvarnished look at sexual addiction, is unabashedly non-academic, and practical. One criticism I have is that some of the ways the author talks about addiction. His definition is likely to lead people not addicted to believe that they are. Those he defines as addicted but are not still have troubling use patterns; I simply find the addiction definition in this book to be outside the bounds of good research. That definition is "deciding not to do something and finding yourself not only doing it, but getting worse" (p 26). Aside from that criticism, chapters are short, accessible, and practical. One won't be bored reading this book. It includes helpful illustrations (maps of brain functions, charts and helpful diagrams). It is also quite readable and inherently interesting. The author's writing style is both engaging, accessible, and hard hitting. Young and older men who follow Jesus will likely connect very well with the material.

Another good book written from a Christian worldview is the popular book by Stephen Arterburn and Fred Stoeker *Every Man's Battle.* [257] They have a workbook in the back of some copies that is a very useful study to teach you on a deeper, spiritual level, why pornography is harmful and how to avoid it. The book is heavy on personal anecdotes, heavy on good advice, and light on research and technical jargon. My best guess is that for men who aren't yet addicted by pornography, this study is likely to be very fruitful. For those who are addicted, it might be a helpful addition to more intensive therapy. The book has sold at least 3 million copies, so some folks must be getting something from it! [258]

Another good book written from a Christian worldview is Steve Gallagher's *At the Altar of Sexual Idolatry.*[259] It is heavy on scriptural references, has a fair number of other references to Christian sources, heavy on wisdom and good advice, and light on research. If that appeals to you, it is likely to be a valuable resource. It may appeal to someone who prefers a bit more intellectual depth in writing than "Every Men's Battle" and who is looking to build skills without a step-by-step plan per se.

Another book for Christians that could be helpful is *Finally Free* by Heath Lambert. The goal of the book is to show readers how to use the power of Jesus to free you from pornography. The book takes a grace-based approach, which will appeal to many people. The writing style is accessible and the book is shorter than most. There are thought questions at the end of each chapter that if earnestly used, could lead to helpful reflection and conditions for change. They could also be the basis for a group study. Lambert takes up the topics of sorrow, accountability, radical measures, confession, marital status, humility, gratitude and a dynamic relationship with Jesus to engage in a fight against pornography. These tools are likely to be useful to someone who follows Jesus. A short appendix is also included giving advice to friends and spouses of someone who needs help breaking free from porn.[260]

The book *You Can Change* by Tim Chester focuses, not surprisingly, on the theme of change. Written from a Christian worldview,

Chester goes through several strategies for embracing personal transformation. Chester does a good job helping the reader assess the reasons he wants to change. The book is heavy on scripture references and quite practical. The many references in the book are almost exclusively from the Bible or from Christian books and articles. It is light on peer-reviewed data, but that is not its focus. Its focus is providing advice to people who follow Jesus who desire to be more like Him. Like many books of its kind, it includes thought questions and exercises for the reader to pursue if desired. It seems to me that it is a particularly good self-assessment guide with processes suggested to initiate, and sustain change in one's life.[261]

A secular resource I think is good is the book, *Treating Pornography Addiction: The Essential Tools For Recovery*, by Dr. Kevin Skinner. Dr. Skinner advises people who believe that they are addicted to pornography and are motivated to break that addiction to go through several initial steps prior to initiating an action plan to quit. The first is defining sobriety. In this stage an individual needs to establish what it means to quit. For example, some make the mistake of swearing off the major object of their addiction (i.e. Internet pornography) but fail to identify less severe triggers that may lead to their use (i.e. going to a sexually themed movie with friends, watching TV shows with sexual content, etc.). The next is defining boundaries. This step involved identifying the situations in which relapse will be likely, for example going online when alone. Next, the establishing goals step involves defining the desired end point. Establishing short, medium, and long-term goals can help motivate someone with early successes to work toward long-term victory. Specific and measurable goals are suggested (spending less time fantasizing, remaining porn-free for 180 days, etc.). A next step is identifying a support team. Breaking addiction is next to impossible to do alone. Having a helpful, encouraging group of people who know your struggles and are willing to walk alongside throughout the recovery process is critical. Next comes forecasting and performing fire drills. The principle here is identifying and then developing a plan of action for when a relapse is most likely to occur. For example, calling a friend when the compulsion is felt to use pornography. After this plan is well thought out, not surprisingly, it is time for it to be acted upon. The most obvious limitation in Skinner's book is that it is was written in 2005 and is not up to date with information about the latest means through which pornography is consumed. Still, it is a helpful tool.[262]

If you are looking for a book about pornography that is written from a psychologist's point of view and is devoid of religious references, a good choice is *In the Shadows of the Net* by Dr. Patrick Carnes and Dr. David Delmonico.[263] They have a very useful self-administered survey to measure one's degree of problematic sexual behavior, which can help a person determine the degree to which their pornography use is problematic. They discuss addiction and compulsion, but enter the topic from a less diagnostic point of view. It has a great balance between wisdom, advice, practical surveys and diagnostic tools. Though it isn't heavy on academic references, scholars wrote the book in an intelligent way. If you are looking for a good secular book that can help you identify and find your way out of pornography, or you are looking to help others do so, this is the one I recommend.

A Critique

One perspective from within the faith-based community that critiques aspects of many faith based approaches to overcoming pornography addiction comes from Dr. William Struthers. When I interviewed Dr. Struthers, the one caution that he gave is that

> "they have a heavy emphasis on purity and they sometimes confuse, at a theological level, the issue of sanctification. They espouse the notion that you are sexually pure, you just have to prevent porn

or affairs from polluting you. Actually that gets it backwards; you begin with a sin nature, you are already impure. Just because you are sexually inexperienced doesn't make you sexually pure. The process of sanctification is about moving forward and getting rid of things along the way, rather than thinking that you are pure and you have to kind of navigate and avoid touching bad stuff. The better notion is to understand yourself, to understand that sex is a good thing, it is not to be avoided; it is to be harnessed in a healthy way that honors the dignity of other people. A lot of the religious groups are about preventing bad stuff. My belief is more of a reformed theology – we are all bad – the goal is to distill that badness, put yourself in a crucible, let those impurities rise to the surface, skim those off the top, and then replace them with better things."

Approaches for Pastors, Parents, and Counselors

Pastors

If you have a leadership role in a church or ministry and if you haven't started fighting the spiritual and cultural battle against pornography, you need to do so now. After talking with numerous men who are living with a porn addiction, I've learned that for them, it is an isolating, shameful, horrific experience. We need the church today to be a place where men, women, boys, and girls can follow the advice in James 5:16, "Therefore, confess your sins to one another and pray for one another, that you may be healed. The prayer of a righteous person has great power as it is working." Too many churches today ignore the problem of pornography, at the peril of their members. Ignoring pornography use in the church is much like pretending that Satan doesn't exist and that all we need to do is try to be good on our own to please God. Both lead to destruction. The church must get past its discomfort with talking about the sin, and focus on praying for and loving the sinner out of that which entraps his spirit. The time for thinking "It doesn't happen in my church" is over. Preach a sermon on pornography, host a "Porn Sunday" program where you blow the lid off the issue, start a support group using the Celebrate Recovery Model or another reputable program, and publicize the availability of counselors in your area who are Christian and certified sex addiction therapists.

The Pornography Trap by Ralph Earle and Mark Laaser is written for pastors and other church leaders. Though it is getting a little dated, given that it was published before Internet pornography took hold, it remains relevant. The book is written to be practical, with a moderate number of biblical references and few scholarly citations. There are brief self-assessment tools and advice that will ring true to pastors and those who work in broader ministry positions. The writing is accessible and the book is briefer than most. For pastors, this is a useful tool.[264]

Parents

Parents need to take the lead on guiding their children away from the messages pornography sends them. There are several ways to do this. If your child is 11 or older, it is likely too late to help them deal with pornography for the first time, but it is never too late to talk to your son or daughter. I recommend starting conversations about pornography around age 9. Asking questions can be a great way to initiate a conversation. Some that I like are:

1. If someone showed you a picture of people who didn't have their clothes on, what do you think you would do?
2. Do you think it is ok to watch videos where people have no clothes on?

3. If you are over at a friend's house and they told you they wanted to show you something cool but that you can't tell your parents, what would you say?

Obviously, the place you want to get with your children is a response where they develop the skills to say to friends "No thanks, I don't want to look at that," or some variation of that phrase. When your children reach the age where they have smart phones (which I think should be as late as possible) and even more importantly when their friends have smart phones, specific conversations with them about what to do when a friend shows them pictures of naked people need to happen. I'd suggest avoiding the term 'pornography' as it can be a vague one. Rather, I'd suggest focusing on pictures of people doing things that should be private; things that we don't have a right to look at.

Another common idea I've heard, and support, is to tell your kids that they can have privacy in two places – in the bathroom and when changing clothes. Otherwise, as their parent, you can and will look into anything they have. Parents should control passwords on phones, should install accountability software, and take phones away if they are being used to access pornography. Bear in mind that when you give kids privacy in bathrooms, that is often a place they will go to look at pornography and masturbate. While it is likely a good idea to give them privacy while using the toilet, you might say something through the door to them if they are in there for an extended period of time and just check in.

The most promising secular resource I am enthusiastic about for parents is one that at the time of writing this book was in the final stages of being completed. A nonprofit organization called Culture Reframed (www.culturereframed.org), led by Dr. Gail Dines, is coming out with an online program for parents and another one for health care providers. Though I have not seen it because it was not completed at the time this book went to print, it should be out at the time you are reading this. In the parent's program, the goal is to help parents build resilience and resistance in kids to the porn culture. The program will be rooted in a series of three-minute videos of good advice for how parents can have conversations with their children. In addition, there will be a helpful tool kit, advice, worksheets, and a complete guide for parents who want (and need) to talk to their kids about porn. Alongside that, Culture Reframed is building a professional's program where they are resourcing therapists, doctors, adolescent psychologists, and pediatricians to provide education on how to best help patients and clients struggling with porn addiction.

Lastly, I asked Dr. Gail Dines for ideas on how parents can help their children avoid the perils of pornography. She noted,

> "Fighting porn is not just about restricting access. You want to get kids to the point where they know that going on that will have an effect on them that they don't want to have. It is not just restricting access, it has to go much deeper than that. Because if you restrict access, any kid can get around a filter. You have to resource the kids to understand that if I click on to this, what is the cost going to be to me? And the cost is that you are going to be manipulated by the porn industry, you are going to be used, they are going to hijack your sexuality before you even own it, they are going to turn you into a commodity, and you are going to lose control over your life."

Counselors

If you are counseling a client who has viewed pornography and he or she wonders if they will be able to perform sexually in the way people in pornography do, it is wise to tell them that they cannot. This is because male performers tend to take drugs to facilitate their sexual performance. Female performers often have breast implants, take drugs to dull the pain, and go to great lengths to pretend they are enjoying what is, in fact, painful. Thus, what is seen in pornography isn't an accurate reflection of what can be expected from a sexual encounter. Counselors (and parents) should also know that many male adolescents view pornography for purposes of sex education. Of course it is natural for adolescent boys (and girls) to be curious about sex and for them to want to know more about it. When they seek such information from pornography, they are likely to see unhealthy, and of course unbiblical, sexual behaviors and practices. The consequences of this can include conflicted views about sexuality, potentially violent beliefs and attitudes toward women, and unhealthy sexual practices. Thus, a counselor should be ready to educate adolescents about both the mechanics of sex, and the emotional elements. In doing so, they should keep in mind that what the adolescent has likely seen portrays a violent, power-imbalanced view of sexual relations rather than a mutual expression of a loving relationship in the context of God's design for marriage.[265]

Counselors should also know that experimental studies involving brain scans show that people addicted to pornography are on a constant quest for novel images, become conditioned and then habituated to the sexual stimuli they masturbate to, usually in private. Such addicted individuals tend to be more anxious, depressed, impulsive, and obsessive-compulsive. Thus, clients or patients who present as anxious or depressed should be asked about their pornography use.[266]

Public Policy

If the grip that pornography has on so many is ever to be loosened, a coordinated public policy effort must take place. This could occur using several different strategies. My hope is that after having read this book, you will be more motivated to work towards changes on a broad, societal level. Below, I mention some ideas that can help make societal change.

Public Health Approach

Dr. Gail Dines, the unofficial leader of the secular anti-porn movement, now believes that

> "The greatest hope in the U.S. for stemming the porn industry is the public health approach. I would like to see violent porn basically restricted to such a degree that it would be very difficult to get ahold of. I'd like to see restrictions to the production side as well because there is terrible violence toward women in it. In the USA, the best model we've come up with is the public health model. It gets traction, it makes sense, it gets to the root of the problem."

According to the American Public Health Association, public health "promotes and protects the health of people and the communities where they live, learn, work and play."[267] This approach seems both logical and promising for addressing the dangers of pornography in the years to come.

Regulate ISPs

Another promising strategy for curtailing the cultural influence of pornography is offered by Dr. Kirk Doran, who suggests that people advocate for regulation of Internet service providers. More than 4 out of 5 people who use the Internet, do so through only 25 service providers. If Internet lines were regulated in the degree to which they could transmit obscene material (and transmitting the obscene is of course illegal), many consumers would be unable to access much of the Internet pornography on the Internet today. Devastating enforcement of any violation of such regulations by ISPs would be essential for this to work.[268]

Take Action Through Organizations

One organization that I have found very helpful for those seeking to have a broad impact in the fight against pornography is the National Center on Sexual Exploitation (endsexualexploitation.org). This group does a great job impacting public policy and getting corporations to end practices that sexually exploit others. For example, they successfully convinced several hotel chains to remove in-room pornography from their guest rooms, worldwide. One reason they are so successful is that they give people like you a voice by giving you easy actions like sending an email to targeted groups when an effort is undertaken. This simple way of demonstrating your support can help make big changes. The direct link to this portion of their work is endexploitationaction.com. They also have a substantial archive of published research, online presentations, and helpful articles for people who seek to decrease the influence of pornography in our society. I highly recommend subscribing to their website, donating to help their work, and helping in any way you can.

A Concluding Thought

A generation has been raised using pornography as a guide to sexual behavior. As many note, the pornography industry has hijacked the sexuality of the generation that has grown up on Internet pornography. They have been sold a lie that sexual intimacy should be violent, impersonal, and demeaning to women. If you are in this generation, I urge you to apply every practice in this chapter that seems helpful to you, and those mentioned in the several books I have recommended, so that you can take back your conception of what a healthy sexual relationship consists of in reality. Without a doubt, the best model of healthy sexuality is articulated by the one who created sex itself, God! Reading Song of Solomon goes a long way to understanding how God designed sex, and how it should be used to bond husband and wife.

I urge you to do all it takes to rid yourself of the lies our pornified culture has sold you. If you have not viewed pornography, you are a rare individual. I urge you to be contagious and get involved in the fight against pornography. If you are concerned about the generation raised on today's pornography and the generations to follow, I implore you to take up the fight to keep pornography from the eyes of those you love. Recognize that the battle is even more than one for individuals; it is for all of us. Participate in efforts designed to remove sexually violent images from your computers, the businesses you give your money to, and the laws passed by those whom you elect. Make every effort to keep sexually violent images from popping up on or otherwise appearing on your Internet accessible devices. Pursue a healthy sexuality, free from violence, free from the influences of an industry that will do anything to anyone to get your money, and free from the messages that sex should hurt and is demeaning, particularly to women. Though it is impossible in today's society not to see pornography, I hope that by implementing the ideas in this and other chapters throughout *How Pornography Harms*, that you will live by your values rather than those of an evil, devastatingly harmful business. In my view, we are better than what the pornography industry makes people out to be. My wish for you, and our culture, is to be free from their influence once and for all.

End Notes

1   Peter, J., & Valkenburg, P. M. (2010). Adolescents' use of sexually explicit Internet material and sexual uncertainty: The role of involvement and gender. *Communication Monographs, 77,* 357–375. doi:10.1080/03637751.2010.498791

2   Bridges, A.J., Wosnitzer, R., Scharrer, E. Sun, C., & Liberman, R. (2010). Aggression and sexual behavior in best-selling pornography videos: A content analysis update. *Violence Against Women, 16,* 1065-1085.

3   Tyler, M. (2010). Now that's pornography! In (K. Boyle, Ed.) *Everyday pornography.* New York: Routledge.

4   Gorman S, Monk-Turner E, Fish J. (2010). Free adult Internet web sites: How prevalent are degrading acts? *Gender Issues, 27* (3-4), 131-145.

5   Boyle, K. (2010). *Everyday pornography.* New York: Routledge.

6   Jensen, R. (2007). *Getting off: Pornography and the end of masculinity*: South End Press Cambridge, MA.

7   DeKeseredy, W. S. & Corsianos, M. (2016). *Violence Against Women in Pornography.* New York: Routledge.

8   Digital Journal (2014) How many Christians do you think watch porn? Available at http://www.digitaljournal.com/pr/2123093 (accessed 16 January 2015).

9   2014 *ProvenMen.org Pornography Addiction Survey (conducted by Barna Group).* The survey results are located at www.provenmen.org/2014pornsurvey/pornography-use-and-addiction.

10   Dines, G. (2010). *Pornland: How porn has hijacked our sexuality.* Boston, MA: Beacon Press.

11   DeKeseredy, W. S. & Corsianos, M. (2016). *Violence Against Women in Pornography*. New York: Routledge.

12   Short, M. B., Black, L., Smith, A. H., Wetterneck, C. T., & Wells, D. E. (2012). A review of Internet pornography use research: Methodology and content from the past 10 years. *CyberPsychology, Behavior & Social Networking, 15*(1), 13-23.doi:10.1089/cyber.2010.0477

13   Wéry, A., & Billieux, J. (2016). Online sexual activities: An exploratory study of problematic and non-problematic usage patterns in a sample of men. *Computers in Human Behavior, 56,* 257-266.

14   Ropelato J. (2010) Internet pornography statistics. TopTenReviews. com. Available at http://Internet-filter-review.toptenreviews.com/Internet-pornography-statistics.html

15   DeKeseredy, W. S. & Corsianos, M. (2016). *Violence Against Women in Pornography*. New York: Routledge.

16   Ropelato J. (2010) Internet pornography statistics. TopTenReviews. com. Available at http://Internet-filter-review.toptenreviews.com/Internet-pornography-statistics.html (accessed November 5, 2015).

17   Hymes, T. (2011). Time Warner cable: Free porn is hurting our bottom line. XBIZ, July 29, 2011.

18   http://www.nytimes.com/1994/04/15/us/tobacco-chiefs-say-cigarettes-aren-t-addictive.html?pagewanted=all retrieved December 10, 2015

19   Atwood, F. & Smith, C. (2014). Porn Studies: An introduction, *Porn Studies,* 1:1-2, 1-6, DOI: 10.1080/23268743.2014.887308

20   Malamuth, N. M., Addison, T. & Koss, M. P. (2000). Pornography and sexual aggression: Are there reliable effects and can we understand them? *Annual Review of Sex Research, 11,* 26-91.

21   Peter, J. & Valkenburg, P. M. (2016): Adolescents and Pornography: A Review of 20 Years of Research, *The Journal of Sex Research*, DOI: 10.1080/00224499.2016.1143441

22   Wright, P. J. (2013). A Three-Wave Longitudinal Analysis of Preexisting Beliefs, Exposure to Pornography, and Attitude Change. *Communication Reports, 26*:1, 13-25.

23   Paul, P. (2010). From pornography to porno to porn: How porn became the norm. In (J.R. Stoner & D. M. Hughes, Eds.). *The social costs of pornography.* USA: Witherspoon Institute Inc.

24   Kimmel, M. (2008). *Guyland: The Perilous World Where Boys Become Men.* Harper: New York.

25 Kimmel, M. (2008). *Guyland: The Perilous World Where Boys Become Men*. Harper: New York.

26 Layden, M. A. (2010). Pornography and violence. In (J.R. Stoner & D.M. Hughes, Eds.) *The social costs of pornography*. USA: Witherspoon Institute.

27 Lastoria, M., & Association for Christians in Student Development. (2011). *Sexuality, religiosity, behaviors, attitudes: A look at religiosity, sexual attitudes and sexual behaviors of Christian college students; a survey study*. Houghton, N.Y: ACSD, Houghton College.

28 Hitchcock, M. (2012). *The End: A complete overview of Bible prophecy and the end of days*. Carol Stream, IL: Tyndale House Publishers, Inc.

29 Digital Journal (2014) How many Christians do you think watch porn? Available at http://www.digitaljournal.com/pr/2123093

30 Baltazar, A., Helm Jr, H. W., McBride, D., Hopkins, G., & Stevens Jr, J. V. (2010). Internet pornography use in the context of external and internal religiosity. *Journal of Psychology & Theology, 38*(1), 32-40.

31 Chelsen, P. O. (2011). *An examination of Internet pornography usage among male students at evangelical Christian colleges*. ProQuest LLC.

32 Foubert, J. D., & Rizzo, A. J. (2013). Integrating religiosity and pornography use into the prediction of bystander efficacy and willingness to prevent sexual assault. *Journal of Psychology and Theology, 41*(3), 242-251.

33 Short, M.B., Kasper, T.E., & Wetterneck, C.T. (2015). The Relationship Between Religiosity and Internet Pornography Use. *Journal of Religion and Health, 54*, 571-583.

34 Hilton, D. L. & Watts, C. (2011). Pornography addiction: A neuroscience perspective. *Surgical Neurology International. 2*, 19. doi: 10.4103/2152-7806.76977

35 Hardy S, Steelman M, Coyne S, Ridge R. (2013). Adolescent religiousness as a protective factor against pornography use. *Journal of Applied Developmental Psychology. 34* (3):131-139.

36 Struthers, W.M. (2011). Pornography and the male brain. *Christian Research Journal, 34* (5).

37 Struthers, W.M. (2011). Pornography and the male brain. *Christian Research Journal, 34* (5).

38 Eberstadt, M. & Layden, M.A. (2010). *The social costs of pornography: A statement of findings and recommendations.* Princeton, NJ: The Witherspoon Institute.

39 Haslam, N., & Loughnan, S. (2014). Dehumanization and infrahumanization. *Annual Review of Psychology, 65,* 399-423.

40 Voon V, Mole TB, Banca P, Porter L, Morris L, Mitchell S, et al. (2014) Neural Correlates of Sexual Cue Reactivity in Individuals with and without Compulsive Sexual Behaviors. *PLoS ONE* 9(7): e102419. doi:10.1371/journal.pone.0102419

41 Wilson, G. (2014). *Your brain on porn: Internet pornography and the emerging science of addiction.* London: Commonwealth Publishers.

42 Banca P., Morris L.S., Mitchell S., Harrison N.A., Potenza M.N., & Voon V, (2015). Novelty, conditioning and attentional bias to sexual rewards, *Journal of Psychiatric Research* doi: 10.1016/j.jpsychires.2015.10.017.

43 Daigle, N. (2010). Acquiring tastes and loves. In (J.R. Stoner & D.M. Hughes, Eds.) *The social costs of pornography.* USA: Witherspoon Institute.

44 Wilson, G. (2014). *Your brain on porn: Internet pornography and the emerging science of addiction.* London: Commonwealth Publishers.

45 Struthers, W. M. (2009). *Wired for Intimacy: How pornography hijacks the male brain.* Wheaton, IL: InterVarsity Press.

46 Wilson, G. (2014). *Your brain on porn: Internet pornography and the emerging science of addiction.* Commonwealth Publishing, United Kingdom.

47 Voon V, Mole TB, Banca P, Porter L, Morris L, et al. (2014). Neural Correlates of Sexual Cue Reactivity in Individuals with and without Compulsive Sexual Behaviors. *PLoS ONE* 9(7): e102419. doi:10.1371/journal.pone.0102419

48 Struthers, W.M. (2011). Pornography and the male brain. *Christian Research Journal, 34.*

49 Wilson, G. (2014). *Your brain on porn: Internet pornography and the emerging science of addiction.* Commonwealth Publishing, United Kingdom.

50 Negash, S., Sheppard, N. V. N., Lambert, N. M., & Fincham, F. D. (2015). Trading later rewards for current pleasure: Pornography consumption and delay discounting. *Journal of Sex Research,* 1-12.

51 Ley, D., Prause, N., & Finn, P. (2014). The emperor has no clothes: A review of the 'pornography addiction' model. *Current Sexual Health Reports, 6*(2), 94-105. doi:10.1007/s11930-014-0016-8

52 Phillips, B., Hajela, R., & Hilton Jr, D. L. (2015). Sex addiction as a disease: Evidence for assessment, diagnosis, and response to critics. *Sexual Addiction & Compulsivity, 22*(2), 167-192. doi:10.1080/107201 62.2015.1036184

53 Hilton Jr, D. L. (2013). *Socioaffective Neuroscience & Psychology, 3*(20767). doi:10.3402/snp.v30.20767

54 Laier, C., & Brand, M. (2014). Empirical Evidence and Theoretical Considerations on Factors Contributing to Cybersex Addiction From a Cognitive-Behavioral View, *Sexual Addiction & Compulsivity*, 21:4, 305-321, DOI: 10.1080/10720162.2014.970722

55 Hilton Jr, D. L. (2014). 'High desire', or 'merely' an addiction? A response to Steele et al. . *Socioaffective Neuroscience & Psychology, 4*(23833). doi:http://dx.doi.org/10.3402/snp.v4.23833

56 Steele, V. R., Staley, C., Fong, T., & Prause, N. (2013). Sexual desire, not hypersexuality, is related to neurophysiological responses elicited by sexual images. *Socioaffective Neuroscience & Psychology, 3*(20770). doi:10.3402/snp.v3i0.20770

57 Hilton Jr, D. L. (2014). 'High desire', or 'merely' an addiction? A response to Steele et al. . *Socioaffective Neuroscience & Psychology, 4*(23833). doi:http://dx.doi.org/10.3402/snp.v4.23833

58 Voon, V., Mole, T. B., Banca, P., Porter, L., Morris, L., Mitchell, S., . . . Irvine, M. (2014). Neural correlates of sexual cue reactivity in individuals with and without compulsive sexual behaviors. *PLoS ONE, 9*(7), 1-10. doi:10.1371/journal.pone.0102419.

59 Laier, C., Schulte, F. P., & Brand, M. (2013). Pornographic picture processing interferes with working memory performance. *Journal of Sex Research, 50*(7), 642-652. doi:10.1080/00224499.2012.716873

60 Kuhn, S. & Gallinat, J. (2014). Brain Structure and Functional Connectivity Associated With Pornography Consumption The Brain on Porn. *JAMA Psychiatry*, doi:10.1001/jamapsychiatry.2014.93.

61 Eberstadt, M. & Layden, M.A. (2010). *The social costs of pornography: A statement of findings and recommendations.* Princeton, NJ: The Witherspoon Institute.

[62] 2014 *ProvenMen.org Pornography Addiction Survey (conducted by Barna Group)*. The survey results are located at www.provenmen. org/2014pornsurvey/pornography-use-and-addiction

[63] Swartout, K.M, Koss, M.P., White, J.W., Thompson, M.P., Abbey, A., & Bellis, A. (2015) Trajectory Analysis of the Campus Serial Rapist Assumption. *Journal of the American Medical Association: Pediatrics*, doi:10.1001/jamapediatrics.2015.0707

[64] Malamuth, N. M., Addison, T. & Koss, M. P. (2000). Pornography and sexual aggression: Are there reliable effects and can we understand them? *Annual Review of Sex Research, 11,* 26-91.

[65] Peter, J. & Valkenburg, P. M. (2016): Adolescents and Pornography: A Review of 20 Years of Research, *The Journal of Sex Research*, DOI: 10.1080/00224499.2016.1143441

[66] Kingston, D. A., Malamuth, N. M., Fedoroff, P., & Marshall, W. L. (2009). The importance of individual differences in pornography use: Theoretical perspectives and implications for treating sexual offenders. *Journal of Sex Research, 46*(2/3), 216-232. doi:10.1080/00224490902747701

[67] Malamuth N. (1981). Rape fantasies as a function of exposure to violent-sexual stimuli. *Archives of Sexual Behavior, 10,* 33-47.

[68] DeKeseredy, W. S. & Corsianos, M. (2016). *Violence Against Women in Pornography*. New York: Routledge.

[69] Layden, M.A. (2010). Pornography and Violence: A new Look at the Research. In J.R. Stoner and D.M Hughes, (Eds.). The social costs of pornography. USA: Witherspoon Institute.

[70] Hald, G. M., Malamuth, N. N., & Lange, T. (2013). Pornography and sexist attitudes among heterosexuals. *Journal of Communication, 63*(4), 638-660. doi:10.1111/jcom.12037

[71] DeKeseredy, W. S. (2016). Pornography and Violence Against Women. In C. A. Cuevas & C. M. Rennison (Eds.), *The Wiley Handbook on the Psychology of Violence* (First Edition ed.): John Wiley & Sons, Ltd.

[72] DeKeseredy W.S. & Schwartz M. (2014). *Male Peer Support and Violence Against Women: The History and Verification of a Theory*. Boston, MA: Northeastern Series on Gender, Crime, and Law.

[73] Thompson, M.P., Kingree, J.B., & Zinzow, H. (2015). Time-Varying Risk Factors and Sexual Aggression Perpetration Among Male College Students. *Journal of Adolescent Health, 57,* 637-642.

[74] Malamuth, N., Hald, G., & Koss, M. (2012). Pornography, individual differences in risk and men's acceptance of violence against women in a representative sample. *Sex Roles, 66*(7/8), 427-439. doi:10.1007/s11199-011-0082-6

[75] Baer, J. L., Kohut, T., & Fisher, W. A. (2015). Is pornography use associated with anti-woman sexual aggression? Re-examining the Confluence Model with third variable considerations. *Canadian Journal of Human Sexuality, 24*(2), 160-173. doi:10.3138/cjhs.242-A6

[76] Bogaert A.F. (2001). Personality, individual differences, and preferences for the sexual media. *Archives of Sex Behavior, 30*, 29– 53.

[77] Malamuth N, Addison T, Koss M. (2000). Pornography and sexual aggression: are there reliable effects and can we understand them? *Annual Review of Sex Research, 11*:26–91.

[78] Hald, G. M., & Malamuth, N. N. (2015). Experimental effects of exposure to pornography: The moderating effect of personality and mediating effect of sexual arousal. *Archives of Sexual Behavior, 44*(1), 99-109. doi:10.1007/s10508-014-0291-5

[79] Wright, P. J., Sun, C., Steffen, N. J., & Tokunaga, R. S. (2015). Pornography, alcohol, and male sexual dominance. *Communication Monographs, 82*(2), 252-270. doi:10.1080/03637751.2014.981558

[80] DeKeseredy, W. S. (2016). Pornography and Violence Against Women. In C. A. Cuevas & C. M. Rennison (Eds.), *The Wiley Handbook on the Psychology of Violence* (First Edition ed.): John Wiley & Sons, Ltd.

[81] Wright, P.J., Tokunaga, R.S., & Kraus, A. (2015). A Meta-Analysis of Pornography Consumption and Actual Acts of Sexual Aggression in General Population Studies. *Journal of Communication.* doi:10.1111/jcom.12201

[82] Waltman, M. (2014). *The politics of legal challenges to pornography.* Doctoral Dissertation.

[83] Malerek, V. (2011). *The Johns: Sex for Sale and the Men Who Buy It.* New York: Arcade Publishing.

[84] http://www.pornhub.com/insights/category/stats, retrieved on December 31, 2015.

[85] Bridges, A. (2010). Pornography's effects on interpersonal relationships. In J.R. Stoner & D.M. Hughes (Eds.). *The Social Costs of Pornography.* USA: Witherspoon Institute.

[86] Bridges, A. (2010). Pornography's effects on interpersonal relationships. In J.R. Stoner & D.M. Hughes (Eds.). *The Social Costs of Pornography.* USA: Witherspoon Institute.

[87] Lambert, N. M., Negash, S., Stillman, T. F., Olmstead, S. B., & Fincham, F. D. (2012). A love that doesn't last: Pornography consumption and weakened commitment to one's romantic partner. *Journal of Social & Clinical Psychology, 31*(4), 410-438. doi:10.1521/jscp.2012.31.4.410

[88] Poulsen, F. O., Busby, D. M., & Galovan, A. M. (2013). Pornography use: Who uses it and how it is associated with couple outcomes. *Journal of Sex Research, 50*(1), 72-83. doi:10.1080/00224499.2011.648027

[89] Wright, P. J., & Randall, A. K. (2012). Internet pornography exposure and risky sexual behavior among adult males in the United States. *Computers in Human Behavior, 28*(4), 1410-1416. doi:10.1016/j.chb.2012.03.003

[90] Wright, P. J. & Tokunaga, R. S. (2015). Men's Objectifying Media Consumption, Objectification of Women, and Attitudes Supportive of Violence Against Women. *Archives of Sexual Behavior,* doi: 10.1007/s10508-015-0644-8

[91] DeKeseredy, W. & Schwartz, M. (2009). *Dangerous exits: escaping abusive relationships in rural American.* New Brunswick, NJ: Rutgers University Press.

[92] Foubert, J.D., Brosi, M.W., & Bannon, R.S. (2011). Pornography viewing among fraternity men: Effects on bystander intervention, rape myth acceptance and behavioral intent to commit sexual assault. *Journal of Sex Addiction and Compulsivity, 18,* 212-231

[93] Brosi, M.W., Foubert, J.D., Bannon, R.S., & Yandell, G. (2011). Effects of women's pornography use on bystander intervention in a sexual assault situation and rape myth acceptance. *Oracle: The Research Journal of the Association of Fraternity/Sorority Advisers, 6(2),* 26-35

[94] Foubert, J. D., & Bridges, A. J. (in press). What is the attraction? Pornography use motives in relation to bystander intervention. *Journal of Interpersonal Violence,* 0886260515596538

[95] Foubert, J. D., & Rizzo, A. J. (2013). Integrating religiosity and pornography use into the prediction of bystander efficacy and willingness to prevent sexual assault. *Journal of Psychology and Theology, 41*(3), 242-251.

96 Cooper, A., Delmonico, D., & Burg, R. (2000). Cybersex users, abusers, and compulsives: New findings and implications. *Sexual Addiction & Compulsivity, 7* (1), 5–29.

97 Waltman, M. (2014). *The politics of legal challenges to pornography.* Doctoral Dissertation.

98 DeKeseredy, W. S. & Corsianos, M. (2016). *Violence Against Women in Pornography.* New York: Routledge.

99 Jensen, R. (2007). *Getting Off: Pornography and the End of Masculinity.* Boston: South End Press

100 Abowitz R (2013) Rob Black, porn's dirty whistleblower, spills trade secrets. *The Daily Beast,* 21 April.

101 Abowitz R (2013) Rob Black, porn's dirty whistleblower, spills trade secrets. *The Daily Beast,* 21 April.

102 Klausner, J.D., & Katz, K (2011). Occupational health and the adult film industry: Time for a happy ending. *Sexually Transmitted Diseases, 38* (7), 649-650

103 Goldstein, B., Steinberg, J.K., Aynalem, G., & Kerndt, P. (2011). High Chlamydia and Gonorrhea Incidence and reinfection among performers in the adult film industry. *Sexually Transmitted Diseases, 38* (7), 644-648.

104 *LA's Condom law sends porn industry packing. The Los Angeles Times. Ted Rall. November 20, 2013.*

105 Kammeyer, K. C.W. (2008). *A hypersexual society: Sexual discourse, erotica, and pornography in America today.* New York: Palgrave MacMillan.

106 Benes, R. (2013). Porn: The hidden engine that drives Innovation in Tech. *Business Insider.* http://www.businessinsider.com/how-porn-drives-innovation-in-tech-2013-7

107 Kammeyer, K. C.W. (2008). *A hypersexual society: Sexual discourse, erotica, and pornography in America today.* New York: Palgrave MacMillan.

108 Pipe, M.E., Lamb, M.E., Orbach, Y., & Cederborg, A.C. (2007). *Child Sexual Abuse: Disclosure, Delay & Denial.* New York: Routledge.

109 Jensen, R. (2007). *Getting off: Pornography and the end of masculinity.* Boston: Beacon Hill Press.

110 Eberstadt, M. & Layden, M.A. (2010). *The social costs of pornography: A statement of findings and recommendations.* Princeton, NJ: The Witherspoon Institute.

[111] Whisnant, R. (2010). From Jekyll to Hyde. In (K. Boyle, Ed.). *Everyday pornography*. New York: Routledge.

[112] Hald, G. M. (2006). Gender differences in pornography consumption among young heterosexual Danish adults. *Arch Sex Behav, 35*(5), 577-585. doi:10.1007/s10508-006-9064-0.

[113] Petersen, J. L., & Hyde, J. S. (2011). Gender differences in sexual attitudes and behaviors: A review of meta-analytic results and large datasets. *Journal of Sex Research, 48*(2/3), 149-165. doi:10.1080/00224 499.2011.551851

[114] Hald, G. M. & Stulhofer, A. (2015). What Types of Pornography Do People Use and Do They Cluster? Assessing Types and Categories of Pornography Consumption in a Large-Scale Online Sample, *The Journal of Sex Research*, DOI: 10.1080/00224499.2015.1065953

[115] Hald, G. M. (2006). Gender differences in pornography consumption among young heterosexual Danish adults. *Archives of Sexual Behavior, 35*(5), 577-585. doi:10.1007/s10508-006-9064-0.

[116] Carroll, J. S., Padilla-Walker, L. M., Nelson, L. J., Olsen, C. D., McNamara, B. C., & Madsen, S. D. (2008). Generation XXX: Pornography acceptance and use among emerging adults. *Journal of Adolescent Research, 23*, 6-30

[117] Wright, P. J., Bae, S., & Funk, M. (2013). United States women and pornography through four decades: Exposure, attitudes, behaviors, individual differences. *Archives of Sexual Behavior, 42*(7), 1131-1144. doi:10.1007/s10508-013-0116-y.

[118] Wright, P. J., Bae, S., & Funk, M. (2013). United States women and pornography through four decades: Exposure, attitudes, behaviors, individual differences. *Archives of Sexual Behavior, 42*(7), 1131-1144. doi:10.1007/s10508-013-0116-y.

[119] Sun, C., Bridges, A., Johnson, J., & Ezzell, M. (2014). Pornography and the male sexual script: An analysis of consumption and sexual relations. *Archives of Sexual Behavior*, 1-12. doi:10.1007/s10508-014-0391-2.

[120] Carroll, J. S., Padilla-Walker, L. M., Nelson, L. J., Olsen, C. D., McNamara, B. C., & Madsen, S. D. (2008). Generation XXX: Pornography acceptance and use among emerging adults. *Journal of Adolescent Research, 23*, 6-30.

[121] Paul, B. (2009). Predicting Internet pornography use and arousal: The role of individual difference variables. *Journal of Sex Research, 46*(4), 344-357. doi:10.1080/00224490902754152

[122] Foubert, J.D. & Bridges, A. J. (*in press*). What is the attraction? Understanding gender differences in reasons for viewing pornography in relationship to bystander intervention. *Journal of Interpersonal Violence. 1-19*, DOI: 10.1177/0886260515596538.

[123] Davis, K. C., Norris, J., George, W. H., Martell, J., & Heiman, J. R. (2006). Rape-myth congruent beliefs in women resulting from exposure to violent pornography: Effects of alcohol and sexual arousal. *Journal of Interpersonal Violence, 21*(9), 1208-1223.

[124] Negash, S., Sheppard, N. V. N., Lambert, N. M., & Fincham, F. D. (2015). Trading later rewards for current pleasure: Pornography consumption and delay discounting. *Journal of Sex Research*, 1-12.

[125] Chickering, A. & Reisser, L. (1993). *Education and Identity*. San Francisco: Jossey Bass.

[126] Struthers, W. M. (2009). *Wired for Intimacy: How pornography hijacks the male brain*. Wheaton, IL: InterVarsity Press.

[127] Sun, C., Bridges, A., Johnson, J., & Ezzell, M. (2014). Pornography and the male sexual script: An analysis of consumption and sexual relations. *Archives of sexual behavior*, 1-12.

[128] Sun, C., Bridges, A., Johnson, J., & Ezzell, M. (2014). Pornography and the male sexual script: An analysis of consumption and sexual relations. *Archives of sexual behavior*, 1-12.

[129] Sabina, C., Wolak, J., & Finkelhor, D. (2008). The nature and dynamics of Internet pornography exposure for youth. *CyberPsychology & Behavior, 11*(6), 691-693.

[130] Carroll, J. S., Padilla-Walker, L. M., Nelson, L. J., Olson, C. D., Barry, C. M., & Madsen, S. D. (2008). Generation XXX. *Journal of Adolescent Research, 23*(1), 6-30.

[131] Struthers, W. M. (2009). *Wired for Intimacy: How pornography hijacks the male brain*. Wheaton, IL: InterVarsity Press.

[132] Skinner, K.B. (2005). *Treating pornography addiction: The essential tools for recovery*. Provo, UT: GrowthClimate, Inc.

[133] Brown, J. D., & L'Engle, K. L. (2009). X-rated: Sexual attitudes and behaviors associated with u.s. early adolescents' exposure to sexually explicit media. *Communication Research, 36*(1), 129-151.

[134] Kaiser Family Foundation. Generation Rx.com: how young people use the Internet for health information. Menlo Park (CA)7 Kaiser Family Foundation; 2001.

[135] Dines, G. (2011). *Pornland: How Porn Has Hijacked Our Sexuality.* Boston: Beacon Press.

[136] Damiano, P., Alessandro, B., & Carlo, F. (2015). Adolescents and web porn: a new era of sexuality. *International Journal Of Adolescent Medicine And Health.* doi:10.1515/ijamh-2015-0003.

[137] Butler, S.M., Smith, N.K., Collazo, E., Caltabiono, L., & Herbeneck, D. (2015). Pubic hair preferences, reasons for removal, and associated genital symptoms: Comparisons between men and women. *The Journal of Sexual Medicine, 12* (1), 48-58.

[138] Lofgren-Mårtenson, L., & Månsson, S.-A. (2010). Lust, love, and life: A qualitative study of Swedish adolescents' perceptions and experiences with pornography. *Journal of Sex Research, 47*(6), 568-579. doi:10.1080/00224490903151374

[139] Bryant J & Brown D. (1989). Uses of pornography. In: Zillmann D, Bryant J, editors. *Pornography: Research advances and policy considerations.* Hillsdale (NJ) 7 Erlbaum; p. 25– 55.

[140] Short, M. B., Black, L., Smith, A. H., Wetterneck, C. T., & Wells, D. E. (2012). A review of Internet pornography use research: Methodology and content from the past 10 years. *CyberPsychology, Behavior & Social Networking, 15*(1), 13-23. doi:10.1089/cyber.2010.0477

[141] Ybarra, M. L., & Mitchell, K. J. (2005). Exposure to Internet pornography among children and adolescents: A national survey. *CyberPsychology and Behavior, 8,* 473–486.

[142] Ybarra, M. L, Mitchell, K. J., Hamburger, M., Diener-West, M., & Leaf, P. J. (2011). X-rated material and perpetration of sexually aggressive behavior among children and adolescents: Is there a link? *Aggressive Behavior, 37,* 1–18.

[143] Alexy, E. M., Burgess, A. W., & Prentky, R. A. (2009). Pornography use as a risk marker for an aggressive pattern of behavior among sexually reactive children and adolescents. *Journal of the American Psychiatric Nurses Association, 42,* 442–453.

[144] Braun-Courville, D. K., & Rojas, M. (2009). Exposure to sexually explicit web sites and adolescent sexual attitudes and behaviors. *The Journal Of Adolescent Health: Official Publication Of The*

Society For Adolescent Medicine, 45(2), 156-162. doi:10.1016/j. jadohealth.2008.12.004.

[145] Peter, J., & Valkenburg, P. M. (2007). Adolescents' exposure to a sexualized media environment and notions of women as sex objects. *Sex Roles, 56*, 381–395.

[146] Peter, J., & Valkenburg, P. M. (2009). Adolescents' exposure to sexually explicit Internet material and notions of women as sex objects: Assessing causality and underlying processes. *Journal of Communication, 59*, 407–433. doi:10.1111/j.1460-2466.2009.01422.x

[147] Owens, E. W., Behun, R. J., Manning, J. C., & Reid, R. C. (2012). The impact of Internet pornography on adolescents: A review of the research. *Sexual Addiction & Compulsivity, 19*(1/2), 99-122. doi:10.10 80/10720162.2012.660431

[148] Casey, B. J., & Jones, R. M. (2010). Neurobiology of the adolescent brain and behavior: Implications for substance use disorders. *Journal of the American Academy of Child & Adolescent Psychiatry, 49* (12), 1189–1201.

[149] Somerville, L. H., Hare, T., & Casey, B. J. (2011). Frontostriatal maturation predicts cognitive control failure to appetitive cues in adolescents. *Journal of Cognitive Neuroscience, 23* (9), 2103–2114.

[150] Owens, E. W., Behun, R. J., Manning, J. C., & Reid, R. C. (2012). The impact of Internet pornography on adolescents: A review of the research. *Sexual Addiction & Compulsivity, 19*(1/2), 99-122. doi:10.10 80/10720162.2012.660431

[151] Wright, P. J. (2014). Pornography and the sexual socialization of children: Current knowledge and a theoretical future. *Journal of Children and Media, 8*(3), 305-312.

[152] Mesch, G. S. (2009). Social bonds and Internet pornographic exposure among adolescents. *Journal of Adolescence, 32*, 601–618.

[153] Cody, G. (2001). *Hardcore from the heart: The pleasures, profits and politics of sex in performance.* New York: Continuum.

[154] Attwood, F. & Smith, C. (2014). Porn Studies: an introduction, *Porn Studies, 1*:1-2, 1-6, DOI: 10.1080/23268743.2014.887308

[155] Palac, L. (1998). *The Edge of the Bed: How Dirty Pictures Changed My Life.* Boston, MA: Little, Brown & Co.

[156] Willis, E. (1993). Feminism, moralism, and pornography. *New York Law School Law Review, 38*, 351.

[157] Liberman, R. (2015). It's a really great tool: Feminist pornography and the promotion of sexual subjectivity. *Porn Studies, 2* (2-3), 174-191.

[158] Williams, L. (1989). *Hard core: Power, pleasure, and the "frenzy of the visible."* Berkeley, CA: University of California Press.

[159] Sun, C., Bridges, A., Wosnitzer, R., Scharrer, E., & Liberman, R. (2008). A comparison of male and female directors in popular pornography: What happens when women are at the helm? *Psychology of Women Quarterly, 32*(3), 312-325. doi:10.1111/j.1471-6402.2008.00439.x

[160] Taormino, T., Shimizu, C.P., Penley, C., & Miller-Young, M. (2013). *The feminist porn book: The politics of producing pleasure.* New York: The Feminist Press.

[161] Moreland, R. (2015). *Pornography feminism: As powerful as she wants to be.* Washington: Zero Books.

[162] Feona Attwood & Clarissa Smith (2014). Porn Studies: an introduction, *Porn Studies,* 1:1-2, 1-6, DOI: 10.1080/23268743.2014.887308

[163] Schawbel, D. (2015). 10 new findings about the millennial consumer. *Forbes.* January 20, 2015.

[164] DeKeseredy, W. S. (2015). Critical Criminological Understandings of Adult Pornography and Woman Abuse New Progressive Directions in Research and Theory. *International Journal for Crime, Justice and Social Democracy, 4*(4).

[165] Peter, J., & Valkenburg, P. M. (2010). Adolescents' use of sexually explicit Internet material and sexual uncertainty: The role of involvement and gender. *Communication Monographs, 77,* 357–375. doi:10.1080/03637751.2010.498791

[166] Peter, J., & Valkenburg, P. M. (2010). Adolescents' use of sexually explicit Internet material and sexual uncertainty: The role of involvement and gender. *Communication Monographs, 77,* 357–375. doi:10.1080/03637751.2010.498791

[167] Dines, G. (2010). *Pornland: How porn has hijacked our sexuality.* Boston, MA: Beacon Press.

[168] Anteveska, A. & Gavey, N. (2015). "Out of Sight and Out of Mind": Detachment and Men's Consumption of Male Sexual Dominance and Female Submission in Pornography. *Men and Masculinities,* 18: 605-629, doi:10.1177/1097184X15574339

[169] Smith, P. K., Thompson, F., & Davidson, J. (2014). Cyber safety for adolescent girls: Bullying, harassment, sexting, pornography, and

solicitation. *Current Opinion In Obstetrics & Gynecology, 26*(5), 360-365. doi:10.1097/GCO.0000000000000106

[170] Strohmaier, H., Murphy, M. & DeMatteo, D. (2014). Youth sexting: Prevalence rates, driving motivations, and the deterrent effect of legal consequences. *Sexual Research and Social Policy, 11*, 245-255.

[171] Internet Watch Foundation in partnership with Microsoft Emerging Patterns and Trends Report #1. Youth-Produced Sexual Content. March 10, 2015.

[172] Wright, P. J., & Donnerstein, E. (in press). Sex online: Pornography, sexual solicitation, and sexting. In V. Strasburger & M. Moreno (Eds.), *Adolescent medicine: State of the art reviews*. Washington DC: American Academy of Pediatrics.

[173] Klettke B, Hallford D, Mellor D. Sexting prevalence and correlates: A systematic literature review. *Clinical Psychology Review*. 2014;(1):44-53

[174] Strohmaier, H., Murphy, M. & DeMatteo, D. (2014). Youth sexting: Prevalence rates, driving motivations, and the deterrent effect of legal consequences. *Sexual Research and Social Policy, 11*, 245-255.

[175] Strohmaier, H., Murphy, M. & DeMatteo, D. (2014). Youth sexting: Prevalence rates, driving motivations, and the deterrent effect of legal consequences. *Sexual Research and Social Policy, 11*, 245-255.

[176] O'Sullivan, L. F., & Ronis, S. T. (2013). Virtual cheating hearts: Extra dyadic and poaching interactions among adolescents with links to online sexual activities. *Canadian Journal of Behavioral Science, 45*(3), 175-184. doi:10.1037/a0031683

[177] Vanderbosch, L., van Oosten, J.M., & Peter, J. (in press). The relationship between sexual content on mass media and social media: A longitudinal study. *Cyberpsychology, Behavior, and Social Networking*, doi:10.1089/cyber.2015.0197

[178] Vanden A, Eggermont S, Roe K, Campbell S. (2014). Sexting, mobile porn use, and peer group dynamics: Boys' and girls' self-perceived popularity, need for popularity, and perceived peer pressure. *Media Psychology, 17*(1):6-33.

[179] Wright, P. J., & Donnerstein, E. (in press). Sex online: Pornography, sexual solicitation, and sexting. In V. Strasburger & M. Moreno (Eds.), *Adolescent medicine: State of the art reviews*. Washington DC: American Academy of Pediatrics.

[180] Crimmins, D. M., & Seigfried-Spellar, K. C. (2014). Peer attachment, sexual experiences, and risky online behaviors as predictors of sexting behaviors among undergraduate students. *Computers in Human Behavior, 32*, 268-275. doi:10.1016/j.chb.2013.12.012

[181] Juniper Research: Tablets are for Porn. *Xbiz*. June 11, 2012.

[182] Tongue, S. (2015). Utherverse: Brian Shuster Looks to the Next Big Wave in Porn. *Xbiz*. October 30, 2015

[183] Tongue, S. (2015). Utherverse: Brian Shuster Looks to the Next Big Wave in Porn. *Xbiz*. October 30, 2015.

[184] Bartow, A. (2012). Copyright Law and Pornography, 91 *Oregon Law Review*, 1. Available at http://digitalcommons.pace.edu/lawfaculty/867/.

[185] Citron, C.K. & Franks, M.A. (2014). Criminalizing revenge porn. *Wake Forest Law Review, 49,* 345-391.

[186] Hart B (2014) *Revenge Porn*. Portland, Maine: Muskie School of Public Service.

[187] Salter M and Crofts T (2014) Responding to revenge porn: Challenging online legal impunity. In Comella L and Tarrant S (eds) *New Views on Pornography: Sexuality Politics and the Law*. Santa Barbara, California: Praeger.

[188] Genn, B. A. (2014) "What Comes Off, Comes Back to Burn: Revenge Pornography as the Hot New Flame and How it Applies to the First Amendment and Privacy Law." *American University Journal of Gender Social Policy and Law 23,* no. 1: 163-195.

[189] Foubert, J.D., Brosi, M.W., & Bannon, R.S. (2011). Pornography viewing among fraternity men: Effects on bystander intervention, rape myth acceptance and behavioral intent to commit sexual assault. *Journal of Sex Addiction and Compulsivity, 18,* 212-231.

[190] Makin, D.A. & Morczek, A.L. (2015). X views and counting: Interest in rape-oriented pornography as gendered microaggression. *Journal of Interpersonal Violence*, doi:10.1177/0886260515573572.

[191] Foubert, J. D., Brosi, M. W., & Bannon, R. S. (2011). Pornography viewing among fraternity men: Effects on bystander intervention, rape myth acceptance and behavioral intent to commit sexual assault. *Sexual Addiction & Compulsivity, 18*(4), 212-231.

[192] Brosi, M.W., Foubert, J.D., Bannon, R.S., & Yandell, G. (2011). Effects of women's pornography use on bystander intervention in a

sexual assault situation and rape myth acceptance *Oracle: The Research Journal of the Association of Fraternity/ Sorority Advisors* 6.2, 26-35.

[193] Brown, J. D., Keller, S., & Stern, S. (2009). Sex, Sexuality, Sexting, and SexEd: Adolescents and the Media. *Prevention Researcher, 16*(4), 12-16.

[194] Hall, J. A. (2016). Interpreting Social–Sexual Communication: Relational Framing Theory and Social–Sexual Communication, Attraction, and Intent. *Human Communication Research, 42*(1), 138-164.

[195] Wright, P. J. (2013). A three-wave longitudinal analysis of preexisting beliefs, exposure to pornography, and attitude change. *Communication Reports, 26*(1), 13-25. doi:10.1080/08934215.2013.773053

[196] Sun, C., Bridges, A., Johnason, J., & Ezzell, M. (2014). Pornography and the male sexual script: An analysis of consumption and sexual relations. *Archives of Sexual Behavior*, 1-12. doi:10.1007/s10508-014-0391-2.

[197] Miles, L. A., Cooper, R. L., Nugent, W. R., & Ellis, R. A. (2016). Sexual addiction: A literature review of treatment interventions. *Journal of Human Behavior in the Social Environment, 26*(1), 89-99.

[198] Price, J., Patterson, R., Regnerus, M., & Walley, J. (2015). How much more XXX is Generation X consuming? Evidence of changing attitudes and behaviors related to pornography since 1973, *The Journal of Sex Research,* doi: 10.1080/00224499.2014.1003773.

[199] Price, J., Patterson, R., Regnerus, M., & Walley, J. (2015). How much more XXX is Generation X consuming? Evidence of changing attitudes and behaviors related to pornography since 1973, *The Journal of Sex Research,* doi: 10.1080/00224499.2014.1003773.

[200] Braun-Courville, D. K., & Rojas, M. (2009). Exposure to sexually explicit Web sites and adolescent sexual attitudes and behaviors. *The Journal Of Adolescent Health: Official Publication Of The Society For Adolescent Medicine, 45*(2), 156-162. doi:10.1016/j.jadohealth.2008.12.004

[201] Carroll, J. S., Padilla-Walker, L. M., Nelson, L. J., Olson, C. D., Barry, C. M., & Madsen, S. D. (2008). Generation XXX. *Journal of Adolescent Research, 23*(1), 6-30.

[202] Price, J., Patterson, R., Regnerus, M., & Walley, J. (2015). How much more XXX is Generation X consuming? Evidence of changing attitudes and behaviors related to pornography since 1973, *The Journal of Sex Research,* doi: 10.1080/00224499.2014.1003773.

[203] Bobkowski, P. S., Shafer, A., & Ortiz, R. R. (2016). Sexual intensity of adolescents' online self-presentations: Joint contribution of identity, media consumption, and extraversion. *Computers in Human Behavior, 58,* 64-74.

[204] Bandura, A. (1991). Social cognitive theory of self-regulation. *Organizational Behavior and Human Decision Processes, 50,* 248-287.

[205] Bridges, A. (2010). Pornography's effects on interpersonal relationships. In J.R. Stoner & D.M. Hughes (Eds.). *The Social Costs of Pornography.* USA: Witherspoon Institute.

[206] Sun, C. Bridges, A., Johnason, J., & Ezzell, M. (2015). Pornography and the male sexual script: An analysis of consumption and sexual relations. *Archives of Sexual Behavior.* doi: 10.1007/s10508-014-0391-2

[207] Morgan, E. M. (2011). Associations between young adults' use of sexually explicit materials and their sexual preferences, behaviors, and satisfaction. *Journal of Sex Research, 48*(6), 520-530. doi:10.1080/002 24499.2010.543960

[208] Wright, P. J. (2012). A longitudinal analysis of US adults' pornography exposure: Sexual socialization, selective exposure, and the moderating role of unhappiness. *Journal of Media Psychology: Theories, Methods, and Applications, 24*(2), 67-76. doi:10.1027/1864-1105/a000063

[209] Wright, P. J. (2012). A longitudinal analysis of US adults' pornography exposure: Sexual socialization, selective exposure, and the moderating role of unhappiness. *Journal of Media Psychology: Theories, Methods, and Applications, 24*(2), 67-76. doi:10.1027/1864-1105/a000063

[210] Malamuth, N. M., Addison, T. & Koss, M. P. (2000). Pornography and sexual aggression: Are there reliable effects and can we understand them? *Annual Review of Sex Research, 11,* 26-91.

[211] Sun, C., Bridges, A., Johnson, J., & Ezzell, M. (2014). Pornography and the male sexual script: An analysis of consumption and sexual relations. *Archives of sexual behavior,* 1-12.

[212] Wright, P. J., Sun, C., Steffen, N. J., & Tokunaga, R. S. (2015). Pornography, alcohol, and male sexual dominance. *Communication Monographs, 82*(2), 252-270. doi:10.1080/03637751.2014.981558

[213] Marston, C. & Lewis, R. (2014). Anal heterosex among young people and implications for health promotion: a qualitative study in the UK. *BMJ Open, 4*(8), e004996-e004996. doi: 10.1136/ bmjopen-2014-004996

214 Bridges, A. (2010). Methodological considerations in mapping pornography content. In (K. Boyle, Ed.) *Everyday pornography*. New York: Routledge.

215 Braithwaite, S., Aaron, S., Dowdle, K., Spjut, K., & Fincham, F. (2015). Does pornography consumption increase participation in friends with benefits relationships? *Sexuality & Culture, 19*(3), 513-532. doi:10.1007/s12119-015-9275-4

216 Braithwaite, S., Coulson, G., Keddington, K., & Fincham, F. (2015). The influence of pornography on sexual scripts and hooking up among emerging adults in college. *Archives of Sexual Behavior, 44*(1), 111-123. doi:10.1007/s10508-014-0351-x

217 Braithwaite, S. R., Givens, A., Brown, J., & Fincham, F. (2015). Is pornography consumption associated with condom use and intoxication during hookups? *Culture, Health & Sexuality, 17*(10), 1155-1173. doi:10.1080/13691058.2015.1042920

218 Voon V, Mole TB, Banca P, Porter L, Morris L, et al. (2014) Neural Correlates of Sexual Cue Reactivity in Individuals with and without Compulsive Sexual Behaviors. *PLoS ONE 9*(7): e102419. doi: 10.1371/journal.pone.0102419

219 Sun, C. Bridges, A., Johnason, J., and Ezzell, M. (2015). Pornography and the Male Sexual Script: An Analysis of Consumption and Sexual Relations. *Archives of Sexual Behavior*. doi: 10.1007/s10508-014-0391-2

220 Doidge, N. (2007). *The brain that changes itself.* New York: Penguin Books.

221 Kinsey, A.C., Pomeroy, W.B., & Martin, C.E. (1948). *Sexual behavior in the human male.* Philadelphia: WB Saunders.

222 Laumann, E.O., Paik, A., & Rosen, R.C. (1999). Sexual dysfunction in the United States: Prevalence and predictors. *Journal of the American Medical Association, 281*(6), 537-544.

223 O'Sullivan, L.F., Brotto, L.A., Byers, E.S., Majerovich, J.A., Weust, J.A. (2014). Prevalence and characteristics of sexual functioning among sexually experienced mid to late adolescents. *The Journal of Sexual Medicine, 11,* 630-641.

224 Mialon, A., Berchtold, A., Michaud, P.A., Gmel, G. & Suris, J.C. (2012). Sexual dysfunctions among young men: Prevalence and associated factors. *Journal of Adolescent Health, 51*(1), 25-31.

225 O'Sullivan, L.F., Brotto, L.A., Byers, E.S., Majerovich, J.A., Weust, J.A. (2014). Prevalence and characteristics of sexual functioning among sexually experienced mid to late adolescents. *The Journal of Sexual Medicine, 11,* 630-641.

226 Mialon, A., Berchtold, A., Michaud, P.A., Gmel, G. & Suris, J.C. (2012). Sexual dysfunctions among young men: Prevalence and associated factors. *Journal of Adolescent Health, 51*(1), 25-31.

227 Wilcox, S.L., Redmond, S., and Hassan, A.M. (2014). Sexual functioning in military personnel: Preliminary estimates and predictors. *Journal of Sexual Medicine, 11* (10), 2537-2545.

228 Armed Forces Health Surveillance Center (2014). Erectile dysfunction among male active component service members, U.S. Armed Forces, 2004-2013. *Monthly Surveillance Monthly Report, 21*(9), 13-16.

229 Capogrosso, P., Colicchia, M., Ventimiglia, E., Castagna, G., Clementi, M.C., Suardi, N., Castiglione, F., Briganti, A., Cantiello, F. Damiano, R., Montorsi, F., & Salonia, A. (2013). One patient out of four with newly diagnosed erectile dysfunction is a young man--worrisome picture from the everyday clinical practice. *Journal of Sexual Medicine, 10*(7), 1833-1841.

230 Damiano, P., Alessandro, B., and Carlo, F. (2015). Adolescents and web porn: a new era of sexuality. *International Journal of Adolescent Medical Health.* doi: 10.1515/ijamh-2015-0003.

231 Layden, M.A. & Eberstadt, M. (2010). *The social costs of pornography: A statement of findings and recommendations.* Princeton, NJ: The Witherspoon Institute.

232 Hewitt, C., & Marcum, C. D. (2016). Child Pornography. *The Encyclopedia of Crime & Punishment.*

233 Ropelato J. (2010) Internet pornography statistics. TopTenReviews. com. Available at http://Internet-filter-review.toptenreviews.com/Internet-pornography-statistics.html (accessed November 5, 2015).

234 United States House of Representatives, testimony of Ernie Allen. Sexual exploitation of children over the Internet: What parents, kids, and congress need to know about child predators: Hearings before the Subcommittee on Oversight and Investigations, of the House Committee on Energy and Commerce, 109th Cong., 2d Sess. (2006)

[235] Ray, J.V., Kimonis, E.R., & Seto, M.C. (2014). Correlates and Moderators of Child Pornography Consumption in a Community Sample. *Sexual Abuse, 26* (6), 523-545.

[236] Seto, M.C. (2006). Child Pornography Offenses Are a Valid Diagnostic Indicator of Pedophilia. *Journal of Abnormal Psychology, 155* (3), 610-615.

[237] Layden, M.A. & Eberstadt, M. (2010). *The social costs of pornography: A statement of findings and recommendations.* Princeton, NJ: The Witherspoon Institute.

[238] (pornhubinsights.pdf Accessed on December 1, 2015).

[239] Babchishin, K.M., Hanson, R.K., & VanZuylen, H. (2015). Online Child Pornography Offenders are Different: A Meta-analysis of the Characteristics of Online and Offline Sex Offenders Against Children. *Archives of Sexual Behavior, 44,* 45-66.

[240] Bourke, M.L. & Hernandez, A.F. (2009). The 'Butner Study' Redux: A Report of the Incidence of Hands-on Child Victimization by Child Pornography Offenders. *Journal of Family Violence, 24,* 183-191.

[241] Smid, W., Schepers, K., Kamphuis, J. H., van Linden, S., & Bartling, S. (2015). Prioritizing child pornography notifications: Predicting direct victimization. *Sex Abuse, 27*(4), 398-413.

[242] Kingston, D. A., Fedoroff, P., Firestone, P., Curry, S., & Bradford, J. M. (2008). Pornography use and sexual aggression: the impact of frequency and type of pornography use on recidivism among sexual offenders. *Aggressive Behavior, 34*(4), 341-351. doi:10.1002/ab.20250

[243] Seto, M. C., & Eke, A. W. (2005). The criminal histories and later offending of child pornography offenders. *Sexual Abuse: A Journal of Research and Treatment, 17,* 201–210.

[244] Sexual exploitation of children over the Internet: What parents, kids, and congress need to know about child predators: Hearings before the Subcommittee on Oversight and Investigations, of the House Committee on Energy and Commerce, 109th Cong., 2d Sess. (2006) (testimony of Ernie Allen).

[245] Innocent Images: Looking back over the years, and overseas. Federal Bureau of Investigation. https://www.fbi.gov/news/stories/2006/february/innocent_images022406 Retrieved December 16, 2015.

[246] Temple J.R., Paul J.A., van den Berg P., Le V., McElhany A., Temple B.W. (2012). Teen Sexting and Its Association With Sexual Behaviors. *Archives in Pediatric Adolescent Medicine*, 166(9), 828-833.

[247] Wolak, J., Finkelhor, D., and Mitchell, K. (2012). Trends in Arrests for Child Pornography Production: The Third National Juvenile Online Victimization Study (NJOV-3). Durham, NH: Crimes against Children Research Center.

[248] Wolak, J., Finkelhor, D. & Mitchell, K. (2011). Child Pornography Possessors: Trends in Offender and Case Characteristics. *Sexual Abuse: A Journal of Research and Treatment 23*(1) 22–42.

[249] Wolak, J.D., Finkelhor, D., & Mitchell, K.J. (2012). How Often Are Teens Arrested for Sexting? Data From a National Sample of Police Cases. *Pediatrics, 129*(1). 2011-2242.

[250] Kingston, D. A. (2016). Hypersexuality Disorders and Sexual Offending. In *Sexual Offending* (pp. 103-118). Springer New York.

[251] American Psychiatric Association. (1994). *Diagnostic and Statistical Manual of Mental Disorders* (4ᵗʰ Ed.). Washington D.C., APA.

[252] Young, K. S. (2008). Internet sex addiction: Risk factors, stages of development, and treatment. *American Behavioral Scientist, 52* (1), 21–37.

[253] Tao, R., Huang, X., Wang, J., Zhang, H., Zhang, Y., & Li, M. (2010). Proposed diagnostic criteria for Internet addiction. *Addiction, 105*, 556–64.

[254] Cooper, A., Delmonico, D., & Burg, R. (2000). Cybersex users, abusers, and compulsives: New findings and implications. *Sexual Addiction & Compulsivity, 7* (1), 5–29

[255] Love, T., Laier, C., Brand, M. Hatch, L, & Hejela, R. (2015). Neuroscience of Internet Pornography Addiction: A Review and Update. *Behavioral Science, 5*, 388-433. doi:10.3390/bs5030388

[256] Roberts, T. (2008). *Pure Desire*. Minneapolis: Bethany House.

[257] Roberts, T. (2008). *Pure Desire*. Minneapolis: Bethany House.

[258] Arterburn, S. & Stoeker, F. (2002). *Every man's battle: Winning the war on sexual temptation one victory at a time.* Colorado Springs: Waterbrook Press.

[259] Gallager, S. (2007). *At the Alter of Sexual Idolatry.* Dry Ridge, KY: Pure Life Ministries.

[260] Lambert, H. (2013). *Finally free: Fighting for purity with the power of grace*. Grand Rapids, MI: Zondervan.

[261] Chester, T. (2010). *You can Change*. Wheaton, IL: Crossway.

[262] Skinner, K.B. (2005). *Treating pornography addiction: The essential tools for recovery*. Provo, UT: GrowthClimate, Inc.

[263] Carnes, P. & Delmonico, D. (2007). *In the Shadows of the Net: Breaking Free of Compulsive Online Sexual Behavior*. Center City, MN: Hazelden.

[264] Earle, R.H. & Laaser, M.R. (2002). *The pornography trap: Setting pastors and laypersons free from sexual addiction*. Kansas City: Beacon Hill Press.

[265] Bloom, Z. D., Hegedorn, W.B. (2015). Male adolescents and contemporary pornography: Implications for marriage and family counselors. *The Family Journal: Counseling and Therapy for Couples and Families, Vol. 23*(1) 82-89.

[266] Banca, P., Morris, L.S., Mitchell, S., Harrison, N.A., Potenza, M.N. & Voon, V. (2016).d, conditioning and attentional bias to sexual cues. *Journal of Psychiatric Research, 72,* 91-101.

[267] https://www.apha.org/what-is-public-health retrieved January 2, 2016.

[268] Doran, K. (2010). Industry size, measurement, and social costs. In J.R. Stoner & D.M. Hughes, (Eds). *The social costs of pornography*. USA Witherspoon Institute.

Printed in Great Britain
by Amazon